HOW AI, 5G, IoT, AND QUANTUM COMPUTING WILL
TRANSFORM PRIVACY AND OUR SECURITY

INSIDE
CYBER

CHUCK BROOKS

WILEY

Published by John Wiley & Sons, Inc., Hoboken, New Jersey.
Published simultaneously in Canada.

For general information on our other products and services or for technical support, please contact our Customer Care Department within the United States at (800) 762-2974, outside the United States at (317) 572-3993 or fax (317) 572-4002.

Wiley also publishes its books in a variety of electronic formats. Some content that appears in print may not be available in electronic formats. For more information about Wiley products, visit our web site at www.wiley.com.

Library of Congress Cataloging-in-Publication Data is Available:

ISBN 9781394254941 (cloth)
ISBN 9781394254958 (epub)
ISBN 9781394254965 (epdf)

Cover Design: Wiley
Cover Image: © JuSun/Getty Images
Author Photo: Courtesy of the Author

SKY10082702_082324

I dedicate this book to my family: my wife, Mary;
daughters, Nina and Tanya; my sister, Joanne;
my in-laws, Bob and Marie;
and especially to my late parents, Dorothy and Norman.
They all have been a real source of inspiration and support for me.

Contents

Preface

My interest in science and technologies as they relate to security was spawned early in my career when I was a staffer for the late Senator Arlen Specter of Pennsylvania. In that role, I covered many security and foreign affairs issues and developed both a passion and expertise for the topics. Then came 9/11 and the world changed. Security and technologies became a top priority for the government, and I was recruited to become part of a start-up called the Department of Homeland Security, specifically with the newly formed Science & Technology Directorate. My focus was on technologies for CBRNE, (chemical biological, radiological, nuclear, and explosives). Cybersecurity, although in its early stages, was part of that threat matrix of technologies to explore.

After DHS, my career took me to the private sector where I continued my work pursuit in the cybersecurity and emerging technologies field. This included various executive roles at Xerox, Rapiscan, and General Dynamics. There is no substitute for real work experience in both government and industry.

In addition, I became a contributor to *Forbes*, and a visiting editor for *Homeland Security Today*. I became a prolific writer and my articles and comments appeared in the *Washington Post*, *Dark Reading*, *Skytop Media*, *GovCon*, *Security Info Watch*, *Barrons*, *The Hill*, *Federal Times*, and others on cybersecurity and emerging technology topics. I continue to write every week.

Then it was time to teach that knowledge and I added the fourth triad of academia to government, industry, and media: first at Johns Hopkins University where I taught a homeland security course, and subsequently for the past seven years at Georgetown University in their graduate cybersecurity and intelligence programs.

As I was researching the topics of emerging technologies on the horizon and their security implications for a graduate course I teach at Georgetown University's Cybersecurity Risk Management Program called "Disruptive Technologies and Organizational Management," I started to see a pattern. Every week there appears to be a breakthrough, or a new application discovered. That was a challenge: how can businesses and consumers get a grip on emerging tech if the pace of change was so rapid and, in some cases, disruptive?

Internet of Things (IoT) devices are expanding exponentially, and technology breakthroughs reported on the news are almost a daily occurrence. As the adage states, yesterday's science fiction is today's science. We are now expanding our capabilities in every area of science, chemistry, biology, physics, and engineering. That includes heightened space exploration, autonomous cars, as well as building smart cities, new manufacturing hubs, nanotechnologies, 3D printing, and now developing artificial intelligence (AI) and quantum technologies.

And the use of computing, both for performance and security, is being heavily affected in good and bad ways by AI, the IoT, 5G, and quantum technologies with an overriding mesh of cybersecurity.

There is almost too much rapidly morphing information to share, but the topics are too important not to try to tackle and inform.

So my approach to writing this book was to be pragmatic, as it is impossible to "boil the ocean" on the aforementioned subject matter areas that are so expansive and evolving. However, understanding the fundamentals of these technologies, trends, and potential can be communicated. So, I decided to write this book as a primer on how to understand and assimilate impactful technologies on the horizon. To provide useful and thought compelling information on the topics. And specifically, how AI, IoT, 5G, and quantum computing will transform our ways of business, communications, privacy, and especially our security.

Unfortunately, all of us are now at risk of cyberattacks in both our work and personal lives. Most of us, especially the younger generation, live on our smartphones. Everything we do and say on social media can become digitally permanent. When we drive our cars, we no longer rely on paper maps but on our GPS. Soon they also may become autonomous. Our lights, heating, ovens, and other IoT devices are connected and integrated into our lifestyles.

And everyone is beginning to realize that AI is going to significantly change our lives for planning, logistics, and predictive analyses. Add soon-to-be quantum technologies to the mix, and the future has indeed arrived. But are we prepared?

Although we may welcome this new world of emerging technologies, understanding the risks and how to help reduce them is the biggest challenge we may face. Every sector and technological connection now needs to be safeguarded.

So, with those realities and experiences in mind, I sought to write a book that could provide guiding information and frameworks for the layperson, scholar, and professional alike. Understanding what is inside of cyberspace is therefore a central theme throughout and that is where it begins.

Starting with the digital ecosystem overview, I break down the chapters sequentially by their thematic technology applications. I set the theme of cybersecurity in the first part of the book, then follow up on the key emerging technologies affecting us throughout the following chapters, and culminate it in a discussion of strategies, solutions, and what the future may bring, but under the backdrop of cybersecurity as the digital glue that brings them all together securely.

I have only touched on a few of Industry 4.0s potential consequences and the societal effects of our new technology era. The good news is that our comprehension of technology and its uses is expanding at an exponential rate as well. However, benefits come with risks; thus, society's actual need is preparation and adaptability. Otherwise, we risk losing control of the potential that technological progress has.

My summaries and descriptions serve only as a springboard for learning about how developing technologies will affect our way of life today and beyond. I hope you'll do more research to dive deeper in the areas and technologies that interest you most.

Let me start that quest for you by setting the table with an overview of the technologies and what constitutes the cybersecurity risks and requirements to adapt to this newly merged physical and digital world.

CHAPTER 1

An Overview of Our Merged Physical and Digital Worlds and Cybersecurity

We are now living in a disruptive era of technological growth known as the Fourth Industrial Era. The merging of digital, physical, and biological systems is referred to as the Fourth Industrial Revolution (4IR), or Industry 4.0. This new period of development is radically changing economies, societies, and industries.

Klaus Schwab, the founder, and executive chairman of the World Economic Forum (WEF), is credited with coining the phrase *fourth industrial revolution*. This idea was first presented in his 2016 book with that name. In it, he talks about how new technologies that are starting to intersect with the digital, biological, and physical worlds—such as artificial intelligence (AI), the Internet of Things (IoT), and robotics—have transformed entire industries, economies, and communities.[1]

We find ourselves depending more and more on the complex web of linked systems and gadgets that support our contemporary existence as the digital fabric of our lives keeps growing. With this Malthusian growth and exponential development of human and technological connectivity comes risk, especially in the cyber digital realm, which is the symbiotic connection between technologies and digital security. It includes innovation, productivity, privacy, and ethics, but cyber digital is most commonly referred to as the cybersecurity element. The complexity of cybersecurity dangers and their worldwide repercussions have significantly expanded in the past few years due to a difficult geopolitical environment and changing technologies.

Emerging technologies are having a wide range of effects on cybersecurity strategies. The overall value of digital transformation for industry and society might reach over $100 trillion by 2025, according to a recent announcement made at the annual WEF gathering in DAVOS.

The announcement touched on the amazing potential:[2]

Examples of societal value generated by digitization include mass adoption of autonomous vehicles and usage-based car insurance, which could save up to 1 million lives a year worldwide by 2025. In the electricity sector, a cumulative reduction in carbon emissions worth $867 billion by 2025 could be achieved through the adoption of digital technologies, principally through smarter asset planning.

The pace of innovation can be illustrated by the fact that, while it used to take Fortune 500 companies an average of 20 years to reach a billion-dollar valuation, digital start-ups are reaching the same milestone in just four years. The research suggests that, once limitations preventing the mass-market commercialization of enabling technologies such as battery storage and wireless charging are overcome, the pace of change could accelerate.

However, the digital transformation of industries comes with risks attached that will require careful management by all stakeholder groups. One such risk is inequality, which could be exacerbated if access to digital skills is not made available to all. Another is trust, which has been eroded by growing concerns over data privacy and security. This will only be overcome with improved norms of ethical behaviour.

As the WEF noted, digital technology and cloud-based platforms are fully being integrated into this emerging ecosystem. It will catalyze a new era of innovation and automation that affects many industries and verticals, including finance, energy, security, communications, and health. This is already happening at a rapid pace as businesses are using public, private, and hybrid clouds and computing is moving closer to the computing edge.

There is little doubt that the COVID pandemic ushered in a new era of exponentially increased digital connectedness, which has altered the security paradigm. Due to the widespread adoption of remote work by many businesses and organizations, as well as the increased interconnectedness of PCs and smart gadgets that are being brought online from all over the world, the digital attack surface has significantly increased. Targets are everywhere for hackers.

The hackers are quite capable and well funded. Most ominous is that various criminal enterprises, belligerent nation-states, and loosely associated hackers are among the increasingly sophisticated cyber threat actors. All companies, regardless of size, are now targets that can be reached, and any breach might jeopardize their operations, reputation, brand, and income streams. This also applies to consumers.

By 2025, the research firm Cybersecurity Ventures estimates that the cost of cybercrime will amount to $10.5 trillion from multi-vector breaches.[3] That is a frightening statistic because it is bigger than the gross national products (GNPs) of most economies of countries on the globe.

Five Reasons for the Increase in Cyberattacks

The increasing frequency and potency of cyberattacks is not surprising. The number of cyber breaches is still rising for several reasons. In this section I share just five of them, but they are key ones to consider.

For one thing, as more people and data go online globally, the surface area for cyberattacks grows. This implies that there will be more chances for malware to infect computers and for targets to become digital. The increasing number of computers and devices people connect to means more opportunities for phishing and distributing malware.

Hackers who are motivated by financial gain tend to target the low-hanging fruit. Working from outside the office has changed the paradigm of cybersecurity by expanding the attack surface area. That led to essentially millions of connected offices. The quick shift to remote work brought about by COVID-19 made businesses' already inadequate cybersecurity readiness profile even worse. The increased attack surface situation increased the temptation for cyber-criminals to exploit weak home office and remote work device defenses through ransomware, spear phishing, credential stuffing, and other illegal methods.

Although the COVID scare has diminished, it is estimated that nearly half the US labor force is still working from home. Home offices are not as protected as the fortified office sites that have more secure firewalls, routers, and access management run by their security teams. So, if you are one of those people working remotely, make sure you have upgraded security on your devices and certainly a backup of your critical data!

Second, the sophistication and skill of cybercriminals have increased, as shown in their cyberattacks. Hacker tools are readily available everywhere, and in addition, cybercriminals are using AI and machine learning tools to automate their attacks. Their attacks are now more deadly, more calculated, and faster as a result. Businesses are no longer protected by obscurity because hackers can now spread malware to anybody and automate vulnerability scans.

The use of ultra-realistic visuals and mimicry has made social engineering and phishing intrusions more accessible. It is more difficult to recognize a phish. The days of receiving misspelled bank emails from princes overseas and being asked to click through to receive money in an account are long gone.

What is even scarier is, according to the Swiss Cyber Institute, 1.5 million new phishing websites are made monthly.[4] It is probably a lot more than that because they have to be detected to be counted.

The basic cyber reality nowadays is that anyone can easily fall for a targeted phish, especially if it pretends to be an email from a higher-ranking employee. CEOs in particular are not immune to clever spear phishes.

Third, hackers and the dark web are more likely to exchange advanced hacking kits and tools. When the bad guys find a vulnerability, they usually spread it quickly throughout their groups. Marketplaces selling "zero-day exploits" have occasionally appeared on the dark web; sadly, it is difficult to shut them down fast enough before significant harm is done. Zero-day exploits are a type of cyberattack that use a security hole in software, hardware, or code that hasn't been fixed yet. This is compounded because many businesses continue to use antivirus software that is outdated and is not patched, even despite efforts to promote cyber hygiene.

Fourth, the emergence of cryptocurrency has made it simpler for criminals to get paid for ransomware. Hackers like to use cryptocurrencies or prepaid bank cards because they are difficult to trace.

And crypto can be a target in itself for hackers. The fact that cryptocurrencies like Bitcoin and others are kept in digital wallets rather than banks has made them targets for hackers. Because these wallets lack the levels or layers of cybersecurity protections required to safeguard the currency owners, they are an ecosystem of easy targets. Hackers can use covert software to mine cryptocurrency on your computer in addition to ransomware.

Fifth, the extreme paucity of qualified cybersecurity professionals in the field has created vulnerabilities and opportunities for criminal hackers. There are not enough skilled cybersecurity workers to handle demand and counterattacks. Both the public and private sectors find it challenging to stay up-to-date with the most recent malware patches and to continuously monitor the ever-evolving threat horizon as the volume and cost of breaches continue to rise. Unfortunately, there does not seem to be light at the end of the tunnel in solving the global shortage of cyber technicians despite many efforts to attract people to the field.

Knowing how to write algorithms and code is undoubtedly part of most cybersecurity career paths, but it goes well beyond that. In addition, it includes aspects of discipline such as thought leadership, policymaking, senior management, compliance, marketing research, intelligence, and technology foraging. Both a will to learn and possessing soft skills are necessary for success in this area. More people need to be encouraged to pursue cybersecurity career pathways.

To increase the number of cybersecurity workers, more must be done to draw women into the field and to retrain veterans to fill skills gaps. My thought is that it would also be wise for government, academia, and industry to put in a great deal of effort to train and invest in Native Americans, who have a long history of supporting national security in government, to develop the next generation of cybersecurity technicians and data analysts from a variety of urban and rural economically disadvantaged areas. I have proposed that in several articles I have written.

Cyber Wake-Up Calls, Breaches, and the Need to Catch Up

We also need a new approach in building cyber defenses with emerging threats. Both business and government cybersecurity efforts have focused on responding to the most current security flaws or threats in recent years. This is a reactive rather than proactive approach, and consequently cyber defenders were always at least one step behind, making it challenging to mitigate the risks.

Many wake-up calls, such as a significant string of sophisticated threat actor intrusions against numerous high-profile targets (such as SolarWinds, Colonial Pipeline, OPM, Anthem, Yahoo!, and many more), have exposed a defective strategy for data defense and operating with a passive preparedness, which has led to a shift in the reactive mindset.

As a consequence of the sharp rise in security breaches and the increased awareness of how crucial IT is to our operations, safeguarding against breaches is now seen as more than just an expense for the company; rather, it is essential to maintaining reputation and business continuity. Both businesses and governments have been taking a more proactive approach to cybersecurity to fix the broken model.

Despite the increasing frequency, sophistication, lethality, and liabilities linked to intrusions, industry management has largely lacked readiness and moved slowly to strengthen cybersecurity. Businesses are facing more and more cyberattacks; therefore, the C-suite needs to act quickly and prioritize asset protection, especially sensitive data. And they need to invest more in both people and resources.

It is a time of transition for many organizations and provides opportunities to fill gaps and change security postures. To consolidate and safeguard data, a lot of businesses and organizations are moving their data from legacy systems to cloud, hybrid cloud, and edge platforms.

We are also experiencing cyber flux. New operational shifts brought about by emerging technologies like 5G, the IoT, AI, and quantum technologies will necessitate new cybersecurity risk management approaches. A major problem is adaptability and scalability to upgrade to new security technologies and processes, given the broad variety of architectures, systems, and jurisdictions. Certainly, this is the right moment for businesses to be proactive in cybersecurity.

In summary, for all the reasons this chapter discussed about growing connectivity and adversarial sophistication of attacks, ultimately, whether you are a corporation or an individual, your cybersecurity posture must adopt a preparedness-based mentality instead of a passive one. Any business, regardless of size, is now a target in the modern digital environment. A breach might jeopardize a company's operations, reputation, brand, and income streams. Or you might be put out of business by just one breach.

Admittedly, it can be difficult to stay on top of cybersecurity concerns because of the rapid pace of digitization and change. This challenge is particularly difficult with the evolving cyber threats and digital convergence, the topic of Chapter 2.

CHAPTER 2

Cyber Threats, Targets, and Digital Convergence

To understand where we are digitally today, it is important to know how it started and get to the roots of the security problems. It started from the digital inception. The internet was created in a government laboratory by the Department of Defense's DARPA (the Defense Advanced Research Project Agency), and corporate vision was responsible for institutionalizing and commercializing it, ushering in a new era of technological and social revolution.

However, it was created to facilitate communications, and security was not given top priority. As a result, it developed more quickly than security procedures and did not adopt preventative measures. Hence it became the Wild West of interconnectivity and risk.

The Root of the Security Problem Explained

Joel Brenner, a former counsel to the National Security Agency sums up the current state of cybersecurity:

> The Internet was not built for security, yet we have made it the backbone of virtually all private-sector and government operations, as well as communications. Pervasive connectivity has brought dramatic gains in productivity and pleasure but has created equally dramatic vulnerabilities. Huge heists of personal information are common, and cyber-theft of

intellectual property and infrastructure penetrations continue at a frightening pace.[1]

The security problem that was apparent from its inception has been exacerbated by an evolving digital ecosystem of convergence and interdependency. Our everyday financial activity, credit cards, and bank accounts are all linked. Even our interpersonal communications via smartphones at social media applications have become a playground for cyberattackers. All of our records—including private medical histories—are shared digitally and managed by algorithms.

These days, we live in an immersive algorithmic environment. Algorithms are generally defined as a mathematical procedure for solving a problem in a finite number of steps. In the context of the developing digital world, each computer program must have algorithms because they are the foundation of many different applications and systems, including search engines and navigation systems. The algorithms are unleashed and multiplying.

Cyber Safety: The Nature of the Problem

It is understandable why there is a digital predicament. The growing interconnectedness and digital commerce across industries have had major ramifications for privacy and security, especially due to vulnerabilities in digital logistics and secure communications. Everything connected online, whether it is devices or people, can be a target of a malicious digital intruder.

At the highest levels, organizations, both large and small, are awakening to the fact that cybersecurity can no longer be ignored or deferred to the IT department or quarterly board meetings. They do so at their peril.

The scarier part is that the digital ecosystem is becoming more precarious day by day. Viruses, ransomware, and other malicious software that affect our digital interface are appearing more frequently because it has become so easy to spread by criminal hackers. The most popular and easy forms of cyberattacks are social engineering, ransomware, insider threats, distributed denial of service (DDOS) attacks, and spear phishing, particularly targeted at corporate executives. Malware is one of the basic tools and techniques used by hackers for exploitation of data breaching. According to the cybersecurity firm Crowd Strike, cloud intrusions jumped between 2022 and 2023 75%; there was a 76% increase in data theft victims named on data leak sites and a 60% increase in interactive intrusion campaigns. Also, the average breakout time for e-crime intrusion activities dropped from 79 minutes in 2022 to 62 minutes in 2023, giving defenders just one hour to reduce the expense and harm brought on by the incursion. The fastest breakout time was recorded at a mere two minutes and seven seconds, leaving defenders with little time to detect or respond.[2]

The reason that the numbers and rates of incursions are going up is because traditional antivirus protections that many businesses have relied on for years are having a difficult time keeping up and can become obsolete quickly with the sophisticated growing threats, plus there are many avenues of exploitation to get around such protections, particularly now with AI.

Hundreds of millions of private records from banks, internet service providers, and retail organizations have been made public in just the last year. Hackers are using these three elements to obtain confidential information from companies. According to Statista, more than 353 million people were affected by data breaches, leaks, and exposes in 2023, all of which were accessed by unauthorized threat actors.[3] Yet industry has been slow to respond to the threats and breach incidents despite ominous statistics.

Speaking at the 2023 Consumer Electronics Show, CISA Director Jen Easterly insightfully stated the reality of the digital ecosystem's vulnerability and the need to be better prepared:

> My main message here is about cyber safety because we live in a world, as you just said, of massive connections where that critical infrastructure that we rely upon is all underpinned by a technology ecosystem that, unfortunately, has become unsafe. And so, it is incredibly important that us, as consumers, that businesses, that all of our partners come together to ensure that we can drive down risk to the nation and make us all safe as consumers.[4]

Cyber Solutions for the New Digital Ecosystem

There is a large global market for AI in cybersecurity that is anticipated to reach $38.2 billion by 2025. This figure incorporates and
illustrates how AI is becoming more and more significant in cybersecurity. It demonstrates that businesses are making significant investments in AI-based defense against cyberattacks and that market
expansion is anticipated in the upcoming years. This is unmistakable
evidence that AI is playing a more and bigger role in cybersecurity
and that for businesses to stay competitive, they must fully use its
potential.

There is a good reason for the increased investments. Eighty-
eight percent of cybersecurity experts think AI will be necessary to
increase the efficiency of security tasks. This data clearly shows that
AI is going to play a bigger role in the battle against cyberattacks. It
is crucial to take this into account when talking about the application
of AI in cybersecurity.

The convergence of AI in cybersecurity defenses and the creation
of next-generation cyber capabilities, such as analytics and predictive
security, will be necessary for securing digital convergence. AI is a
logical set of tools and the best hope for defenders operating in an
asymmetrical threat environment who are already understaffed and
mostly underbudgeted.

Growing threats are shaping the path for the need for AI. The
digital risk landscape is ever-changing, whether it is due to nation-
state attacks, supply chain threats, or advancements in artificial intelligence. Organizations need to stay up-to-date with threat actors,
especially those involved in vital infrastructure. Yet, complex networks with those IT and OT (operational technology) environments
lack technologies to protect both domains; moreover, a cybersecurity
skills gap makes it difficult for organizations to find the right professionals to protect their systems and secure critical infrastructure
environments.

Because of on-premises systems, cloud computing, and edge
computing, the total IT perimeter for many businesses and institutions has become more complicated and distributed, calling for
improved threat detection, analysis, and incident response as well as
increased visibility. Improved information sharing, hardware, software, training, and protocol capabilities will also be necessary to

counteract the wide range of potentially harmful digital actions. The state of vulnerabilities, compromises, and costs are already evident in cybersecurity statistics, as shown in the following list.

Some Cybersecurity Fast Facts[5]

- There were 2,365 cyberattacks in 2023 with 343,338,964 victims.
  - 2023 saw a 72% increase in data breaches since 2021, which held the previous all-time record.
- A data breach costs $4.45 million on average.
- Email is the most common vector for malware, with about 35% of malware delivered via email in 2023.
- Ninety-four percent of organizations have reported email security incidents.
- Business email compromises accounted for $2.7 billion in losses in 2022.

The threat to industry from cyber incursions and breaches is extracting a cost that is hurting commerce and pushing the costs of operations to consumers. Data breaches affecting the digital ecosystem and the statistics mentioned should serve as a wake-up call that complacency in not an option anymore.

CHAPTER 3

Common Cyber Threats and Defensive Tools

What are the most common cyber threats and defensive tools to intercept them? Cyberattacks come in many shapes and forms. This chapter explores some of the most prevalent types used to exploit and breach data and networks. It applies both to businesses and consumers because the attacks are evolving in volume and capability as we depend on digital operations in both our personal and work lives.

Consider that the intricate web of interconnected systems and gadgets that support our contemporary life is becoming more and more necessary as the digital fabric of our lives grows. We put ourselves at risk from an expanding range of cyber threats, though, with each new piece of technology we add to our houses, each app we download to our phones, and each piece of data we trust to the cloud. To prosper, we need to understand the threats and the tools used to combat them.

The following is an excerpted and useful list of 20 common types of cyber threats compiled by the cybersecurity firm Fortinet. I will delve deeper into some of those threats as we delve deeper into the chapter.

Top 20 Most Common Types of Cybersecurity Attacks

Following is a short list of common cyberattacks. There are even more ways to exfiltrate data by hackers, but for most businesses and consumers, this generic list is a fundamental one to know.

- Malware-based attacks
- Phishing attacks
- Ransomware
- Man-in-the-middle attacks
- Denial of Service attacks (DDoS)
- Brute force attacks
- SQL injection attacks
- DNS tunneling
- Zero-day exploits
- DNS spoofing
- Session hijacking
- URL manipulation
- Inside threats

■ ■ ■

When discussing any cyber threats it is prudent to look at the how, what, and what aspects. For the hacker, it begins with identifying and target and using social engineering to plan a mode of attack.

Social Engineering and Identity Theft

In a nutshell, social engineering is the art of taking advantage of human psychology to manipulate people into defeating formal or informal security safeguards. It is used instead of technical hacking methods to access networks, data, or buildings. By targeting you, your sensitive data, and your identifiable habits, hackers incorporate strategies and tools to use or compromise your identity, often for financial purposes.

It is easy for hackers to do, and it works. Increasingly sophisticated social engineering is an obvious explanation for the rise in identity fraud cases. Instead of using technical hacking methods to access networks, data, or buildings, social engineering is the art of taking advantage of human psychology.

Our increased connectivity, combined with oversharing private aspects of our lives, makes us more noticeable to those attempting to get into our accounts and steal our identities, as well as more susceptible to their attacks.

It is a hacker's paradise with so many targets at their disposal. The Internet of Things, wearable technology, and cell phones have all significantly increased the surface of the threat landscape and the data to be garnered from them. Furthermore, it is difficult for most people to secure those laptops, notebooks, social media apps, and mobile devices from a hacker's prying eyes and keyboards.

Depending on the threat actors and their level of competence, hackers and scammers use a variety of methods. However, identity theft does not have to be complicated, especially considering the easy targets that thieves can target.

One favorite method of obtaining personal information is phishing. Usually, this is accomplished by using a phony website that is made to resemble the real one. The goal of this attack is to steal the victim's identity by tricking the user into entering their username and password into a fictitious login form. Hackers can easily impersonate individuals you might know, banks, and websites with well-known brands. The days of receiving emails from overseas that are riddled with typos and claim to have inherited money are long gone.

Surely, identity threat has been exacerbated by the growing use of social media. The world can see who our friends are, our whereabouts, employment history, buying habits, hobbies, and interests. For the bad guys, it is a means of getting information for phishing or virus campaigns.

I have been a victim myself. No one is invulnerable. People have cloned my accounts and impersonated me on Facebook, LinkedIn, and Twitter, in my experience. Fortunately, I quickly became aware of the hoax. Everyone who uses the internet is vulnerable. Individuals who share their social lives on digital platforms like Facebook,

Instagram, Snapchat, and other networks are at risk of fraudsters obtaining their personal information with ease. This information can then be used to evade security measures or deceive people through social engineering.

Currently, the best defense against social engineering attacks is user education and layers of technological defenses to better detect and respond to attacks. Identity theft cannot completely be prevented, but there are steps that individuals and organizations can take to lessen the risks. This analysis pertains to cybersecurity and the digital component of social engineering. Physical social engineering is often used in crime. I compiled these recommendations from practical experience and many of my presentations. They are easy to do and do not require major financial costs.

The following list provides a summary of four steps you can take to safeguard your accounts, privacy, and reputation:

- **Make secure passwords.** Hackers are very skilled at figuring out passwords, especially if they know your birthdate, favorite phrases, and the street names of previous residences. Frequently changing your password can make their tasks more difficult.
- **Keep a separate computer that you use exclusively for financial activities.** Additionally, if you are always on the go, think about hardware-separated devices that offer protection for distinct business and personal use.
- **If sensitive information needs to be protected, think about using encryption software.** Install virtual private networks as well for an additional degree of protection when using mobile devices.
- **Extremely crucial: keep a constant eye on your social media accounts, financial statements, and credit scores.** Account notifications from Life Lock and other respectable monitoring companies are highly beneficial in raising awareness. It is easier to deal with identity theft–related problems the sooner you identify fraud.

Phishing

Phishing is a popular hacker's tool of choice as most cyber breaches involve some form of social engineering, primarily via phishing.

A targeted phish can fool anyone, particularly if it poses as a personal email from a higher-ranking employee or from a bank, company, or website you frequently visit. Phishing is used by hackers to distribute malware or steal your important data. Phishing software typically arrives in email attachments, but it can also be encountered when you are online.

These days, phishes can be quite complex. The images used to imitate emails or texts from banks, businesses, jobs, and even friends are much more sophisticated than the poorly typed phishing attempts from 10 years ago, and the tools are available on the dark web. Furthermore, thousands of these phishes are sent automatically with the use of machine learning algorithms that can target potential victims and personas from databases from both open sources and the dark web.

Spoofing with phishing is the practice of someone impersonating you or an entity to obtain confidential information, accounts, or data. Usually, it is done by text or email that seems like it comes from your bank or place of employment, or it may be a favorite seller like Microsoft or Amazon. It is common for malware and ransomware to be downloaded when you fall for a spoof. Spoofs used to be simple to identify due to typos, shoddy artwork, and implausible appeals. With the advancement of technology and the skill of threat actors, who can fool anyone, this has altered. Spoofing can occur through messages, emails, websites, and even IP spoofing.

There are the four main common types of phishing:
- **Spear phishing.** Spear phishing aims to obtain sensitive information or access computer systems by sending personalized messages via email, text, or phone. Attackers using this method frequently leverage information from social media, public databases, or previous breaches to enhance their credibility. Spear phishing is spoofing that is frequently aimed at company executives.
- **Whaling.** Whaling targets senior or high-profile employees, such as chief executives and financial officers. Attackers craft highly personalized, convincing messages to extract an organization's sensitive information and data.
- **Vishing.** Vishing entails making phone calls or leaving voice messages while pretending to be a reputable source. The aim

is to exploit personal information, access bank accounts, and steal money.

♦ **Email phishing.** Email phishing attempts to steal sensitive information by email. Attackers pose as legitimate organizations and can target mass audiences.

Phishing is easy and effective: 74% of account takeover attacks start with phishing. The most targeted companies for phishing scams are as follows:[1]

♦ Microsoft (33%)
♦ Amazon (9%)
♦ Google (8%)
♦ Apple (4%)
♦ Wells Fargo (3%)
♦ LinkedIn (3%)
♦ Home Depot (3%)
♦ Facebook (3%)
♦ Netflix (2%)
♦ DHL (2%)

Although phishing is difficult to guard against, there are steps to make phishing less successful. Consumers can protect themselves against phishing attacks, even if they are sophisticated ones. It is possible to identify and stop the effects of a phishing attack in several ways. Here are five useful hints:

♦ **Maintain a secure password.** For each account you have, use a long, different, and distinctive password. Do not disclose them to anybody; instead, store them safe in a password organizer. Changing your passwords frequently is also a smart idea.
♦ **Put antivirus software on the gadgets you use.** Email filters, firewalls, and anti-spyware software fall under this category. Keep these up-to-date.
♦ **Apply common sense when it comes to internet safety.** Do not open links from unknown senders or hidden links, be cautious when responding to emails and messages from

unknown senders, and if you believe there may be a problem with your account, contact the service rather than depending just on one message or link.

◆ **Make sure your accounts are secured right away if you believe you have fallen victim to a phishing scam.** In addition to changing your passwords and reporting the incident, you should closely monitor your accounts for any odd behavior.

◆ **Use multifactor authentication.** By adding extra layers of security, scammers will find it more difficult to obtain all the information needed to access your data.

I am a fan of using lists for cybersecurity risk steps because they are easy to keep and follow. This book has several cyber grocery lists to use and retain.

Ransomware

One of the most frightening cyber threats out there is ransomware. It can destroy your sensitive personal data and ruin a business overnight. Ransomware is also often a product of social engineering and is combined with phishing as a means of delivery to the hacker's target. In ransomware attacks, hackers encrypt important files that prevent the victim from accessing their data. The hackers will use this illegal extortion technique to demand ransom from their victims, after which they will guarantee the restoration of systems and data.

A ransomware attack can frequently destroy a business's networks and systems while also spreading fear and confusion. Particularly vulnerable are businesses and organizations whose operations rely on supply chain coordination and logistical planning. The purpose of ransomware software is to quickly propagate throughout the computers and networks of a corporation or organization.

Ransomware attacks have become an increasingly common occurrence for businesses. Typically, a ransomware assault encrypts the data of its victims and then demands payment, typically in cryptocurrency, before releasing the data. When criminal gangs use encryption to obtain confidential company information, they frequently threaten to make the information public or sell it openly in dark web forums.

Attacks using ransomware have become far more common in recent years, and cybersecurity teams continue to be concerned about them. Per the Verizon 2023 Data Breach Investigations Report, ransomware assaults accounted for 10% of all breaches in 2021 and more than 24% in 2023, up from just under 2% of all breaches in 2017.[2]

Because they lack cybersecurity experience and substantial security resources, small enterprises, health care facilities, and higher education facilities are the most vulnerable industries to ransomware cyberattacks. Although it is not advised, they have paid a heavy price and often secretly pay out ransoms to avoid liabilities and suffering closures.

More recently, there have been other ransomware attacks on bigger well-known targets, like Colonial Pipeline, whose hack caused supply chains and fuel to be disrupted throughout the US Eastern corridor. Others have used similar strategies in targeting meat processing facilities, water processing facilities, and important city services.

The surge in 2023 in the activities of ransomware perpetrators targeted prominent establishments and vital infrastructure such as government offices, hospitals, and schools. The widely used file transfer program MOVEit was the target of significant ransomware supply chain assaults that affected organizations like British Airways and the BBC. Due to this and other attacks, ransomware groups have surpassed $1 billion in cryptocurrency payments that they have demanded from victims, an unprecedented milestone.

Events of the previous year demonstrate how this cyber threat is constantly changing and how it is having an increasingly significant effect on international organizations and security in general.[3]

Concerningly, ransomware and DDOS attacks are becoming more common and more sophisticated. The increasing prevalence of cyber threats to corporate operations and reputation can have a direct impact on a company's capacity to remain viable. Many businesses that are attacked online don't make it to the end of the year. Sixty percent of UK small businesses shut down within six months of a cyberattack.[4]

According to a recent Accenture survey, ransomware criminals are becoming more daring and proficient in their attacks against IT (information technology) and OT (operational technology) settings.[5]

IT focuses entirely on data, whereas OT is more concerned with the actual hardware that drives industrial operations and procedures. They can function apart from one another, as they have for a long time, yet they frequently converge.

As per the research, criminal organizations collaborate and exchange commercial hacking instruments (such as the Cobalt Strike virus that is being pirated) through the dark web. Critical infrastructure industries like manufacturing, finance, energy, and agriculture are among their targets. The report also claims that to increase the repercussions of an infection, hackers are employing increasingly forceful high-pressure techniques, and they frequently use several pressure points simultaneously to demand ransom payments. They also occasionally use threats of double and triple extortion.

The threat posed by ransomware is not new; it has existed since at least the new millennium.[6]

Hackers do not necessarily need to use the most advanced and recent malware to succeed. For a hacker, it is simple to do. They typically rely on the most vulnerable target at the right moment, especially given how simple it is to launch an internet attack.

The National Cyber Security Centre (NCSC) of the United Kingdom has released research announcing that ransomware is among the many dangers that will grow in number and impact over the next two years. The NCSC also noted that malevolent attackers are already using artificial intelligence (AI).[7]

The UK's espionage, security, and cyber agency, Government Communications Headquarters (GCHQ), includes the NCSC, which evaluates how AI has made it possible for inexperienced hackers to "carry out more effective access and information gathering operations . . . by lowering the barrier of entry to novice cybercriminals, hacker-for-hire and hacktivists." The NCSC also warned that by 2025, it believes "Generative AI and large language models (LLMs) will make it difficult for everyone, regardless of their level of cyber security understanding, to assess whether an email or password reset request is genuine, or to identify phishing, spoofing or social engineering attempts."[8]

There are ways to lessen the effects of ransomware. The main requirement is that software vulnerabilities be patched and updated regularly. Regrettably, a lot of businesses and institutions apply updates slowly or even negligently for patching that might stop breaches by criminal hackers.

Hackers have stepped up their illegal activity even more as long as victims pay them. Paying a ransom in reaction to a ransomware assault is not something that the FBI supports. Recovering your data is not a given just because you or your company paid a ransom. In addition, it gives offenders a motivation to seek further victims and incentivizes others to engage in similar illicit activities.

The FBI recommends five steps to help avoid being a victim of ransomware: [9]

- ◆ Keep operating systems, software, and applications current and up-to-date.
- ◆ Make sure antivirus and anti-malware solutions are set to automatically update and run regular scans.
- ◆ Back up data regularly and double-check that those backups were completed.
- ◆ Secure your backups. Make sure they are not connected to the computers and networks they are backing up.
- ◆ Create a continuity plan in case your business or organization is the victim of a ransomware attack.

Unfortunately, ransomware is here to stay as long as hackers can make money through extortion and other means.

Botnets

What exactly is a botnet? According to US Department of Commerce NIST Security Resource Center, *botnet* is formed from the words *robot* and *network*.[10]

Cybercriminals use special Trojan viruses to breach the security of several users' computers, take control of each computer, and organize all the infected machines into a network of bots that the criminal, called a *bot herder*, can remotely manage. They use the hacked computers to launch assaults to crash a target's network, injecting malware, obtaining login credentials, or carry out CPU-intensive operations. Another name for a botnet is a *zombie army*.

Bots are any single devises that are part of a network controlled by hackers that can spread malware and/or ransomware to devices and can be self-perpetuating and destructive, much like a biological virus. A more complex illustration of the capabilities of a bot net may be seen on Technolopedia (https://technolopedia.com/).

Botnet attacks are not new, but because they are frequently automated, they have become more frequent and destructive. Anticipate additional bot attacks in 2025. Bots are employed as cyber threat instruments by both organized crime hacking groups and state-sponsored intelligence entities.

Attackers frequently target systems that are not protected by firewalls or antivirus programs. Although there are several ways for a botnet manipulator to take over a computer, they usually do it by using worms or viruses. Hackers use botnets to execute coordinated DDoS attacks, and they are also employed by organized crime to transmit phishing attacks or spam, which is subsequently used to steal identities.

Typically, botnets are made up of many internet-connected PCs and other devices that are part of a network that hacker's control. Similar to a biological virus, a bot can propagate malware and/or ransomware to devices, which can be dangerous and self-replicating. Through web servers, network bridges, Wi-Fi routers, and antivirus software, attackers frequently target machines that are not protected by firewalls and/or antivirus software. Bots impersonate actual users to steal personal identified information, overload systems, scrape IP, and do other malicious activities.

Although there are several ways for a botnet manipulator to take over a computer, they usually do it by using worms or viruses. Cyber-criminals typically employ brute force, phishing, DDoS attacks, and credential stuffing.

Regrettably, malicious hackers have easy access to a plethora of tools, such as key logger software for password theft and the previously mentioned phishing attacks, which may be used to steal identities by posing as legitimate businesses. Botnets are another effective tool that hackers use to mine cryptocurrency from unwary PCs, taking electricity and bandwidth. On the dark web and hacker forums, a large number of these more harmful botnet tools are freely marketed and distributed.

"Botnets have become particularly and increasingly damaging and costly to the digital economy," according to a report by the Council to Secure the Digital Economy.[11]

Although botnets are already a persistent threat, the potential for botnet assaults to cause more harm is being affected by emerging technologies. AI and machine learning have advanced to the point where bots can now easily automate and quickly extend cyberattacks.

Intelligent botnets that can coordinate assaults, avoid detection, and adjust to changing conditions can be created with the use of (AI). These AI-powered botnets are a serious concern because they may be used to launch large-scale attacks against specific systems, credential stuffing, and DDoS attacks. To make matters worse on the threat meter, cybercriminals are now also using an increasingly popular Bot-as-a-Service to outsource attacks.

DDoS Attacks

Even though there are many distinct kinds of botnets available, DDoS-style attacks are still regarded as the most frequent threat. In a DDoS, assault happens when an adversary uses many devices to send a large amount of traffic to a target system, network, or website. By overloading the target's processing power, this method prevents authorized users from accessing it.

In DDoS attacks hackers exploit typical network device and server behaviors, frequently focusing on the networking equipment that connects to the internet. Attackers thus concentrate on edge network components (such as switches and routers) as opposed to specific servers. A DDoS attack overloads the network's pipe or the bandwidth-supplying devices. Additionally, criminals use DDoS as a service platform to initiate attacks against corporate websites and demand ransom payments, threatening to degrade the service if payment is not made.

Research by communications infrastructure provider Zayo Group found that that in 2023, a DDoS assault typically lasted 68 minutes. Given that affected firms had to pay out $5,896 (£4,700) every minute on average, this translates to an average cost of $407,727 (£325,000) for each attack. The trend is upward as there were 200% more attacks in the first half of 2023 than there were in all of 2022.[12] With more devices online and more connectivity to networks, that is a trend that is likely to continue.

■ ■ ■

In summary, there are many cyber threats to be concerned about and, more important, prepare to defend against. To do so it helps to be threat aware. A useful tool for staying on top of cyber threats is DHS CISA. This organization systematically gathers and disseminates information about the most recent threats, exploits, and cybersecurity vulnerabilities, arming our country with the means to counter these attacks. Businesses, governmental entities, and other organizations can benefit from the cybersecurity information and best practices offered by CISA (https://www.cisa.gov/topics/cyber-threats-and-advisories).

The next step is to know what those cyber threats are targeting and why and how hackers seek potential victims. It usually comes down to who will be the easiest to breach and who will pay for getting their data back. Software supply chains often meet that criteria.

CHAPTER 4

Cyber Threat Targets

Software Supply Chains

The software supply chain has proven to be a major target for cyberattacks in the last few years. Supply chain attacks, which compromise upstream contractors, systems, firms, and suppliers, have been a staple of classical espionage and signals intelligence operations. They are quite successful; nation-state actors use human intelligence to get into the weakest points in the chain and implant malware through coercion or compromise during manufacturing or distribution.

The Colonial Pipeline and SolarWinds breaches, among many others, have brought supply chain attacks to light. Protecting any business or organization from the wide range of cyberattacks is a difficult challenge, but it becomes even more difficult when they are a part of a supply chain involving other parties or vendors.

And supply chain attacks are growing in number. There were 242 reported supply chain assaults in the United States in 2023. This figure has been the highest on record and will likely continue to grow. Overall, between 2022 and 2023, supply chain attacks increased by 115% year over year.[1]

Part of the increase is due to workers operating from home. After the COVID-19 lockdowns were lifted, 40% of the workforce have continued to work remotely. Even though remote collaboration tools can provide some security, remote workers lose the effectiveness of the in-office security umbrella operated by IT with the expertise and the in-office security policies they implement.

While at home, workers might not think about the company's security procedures. Many people use their personal laptops for professional reasons frequently, and to speed up their PC performance, they may disable their antivirus, firewall, and endpoint detection and response software, or browse unsafe websites. They might not be using a secure VPN or upgrading patches, either.

The weakest point of entry will always be sought after by cyber-criminals, so reducing third-party risk is essential to cybersecurity, but that is not always an easy task. Cyberattacks on supply chains may be carried out by nation-state enemies, spies, lawbreakers, or hacktivists. Their objectives are to exploit suppliers, companies, contractors, and weak points in the supply chain. Furthermore, supply chain risk can include both devices and people as well as software for exploitation by hackers. This is frequently accomplished via infiltrating networks with compromised or fake hardware and software, taking advantage of suppliers' lax security procedures, or using insider threats.

It is a problem for all firms to ensure that the supply chain, which includes the design, manufacturing, production, distribution, installation, operation, and maintenance elements, is not compromised. Risk to third parties—the consumers of the goods or services—is especially concerning. The current strategy for ensuring the integrity of the chain is through the use of cybersecurity tools to close operational gaps and by conducting vulnerability assessments. But often those security measures are not followed or are not strong enough to prevent breaches. More focus needs to be placed on risk mitigation and readiness, particularly on endpoint and mobile application security, as supply chain and third-party breaches increase. Each and every business faces the task of making sure that the supply chain—which includes design, manufacturing, production, distribution, installation, operation, and maintenance elements—is not compromised. The infamous SolarWinds attack was successful because hackers took advantage of the operational gaps created by a vast, intermixed, supply chain of technology vendors that had not undergone sufficient vulnerability assessments.

In addition to established standards and oversight, companies need to be aware of every vendor in the supply chain. An industry-backed and government-endorsed framework for supply chain security has been proposed by NIST, the nonregulatory body of the US Department of Commerce, which discusses good practices to address supply chain risks. As advised by NIST:[2]

- ◆ Get stakeholder consensus when identifying, establishing, and evaluating cyber supply chain risk management procedures.
- ◆ Determine the sources, order them, and evaluate both internal and external suppliers.
- ◆ To meet the objectives of supply chain risk management for your company, draft contracts with suppliers and outside parties.
- ◆ Use test findings, audits, and other evaluation methods to regularly evaluate vendors and outside partners.
- ◆ Make sure suppliers and outside providers can react to and recover from service disruptions by completing testing.

In order to protect sensitive and private data from advanced persistent threats (APT), the US Department of Defense (DOD) has developed the Cybersecurity Maturity Model Certification (CMMC) standard. CMMC is based on the NIST body of work, specifically NIST SP 800–171 and NIST SP 800–172. It is going through updates and approval, but CMMC will require additional certifications for vendors seeking to do business with the Pentagon.

With the help of the CMMC standard, companies can assess their computing ecosystem and improve their supply chain resilience capabilities. Business supply chain considerations include these questions:

- ◆ Are supply chain risks prioritized by the organization?
- ◆ Are there workable service-level agreements in place at the company that outline and permit the handling of supply chain incidents?

It is good that the government and industry are reviewing and enacting safeguards into vulnerable supply chains.

Internet of Things and Mobility

Security researchers are placing an increasing amount of emphasis on defending the Internet of Things (IoT) networked IP-enabled smart and non-smart devices from cyberthreats like ransomware, malware, phishing, botnets, zero-day exploits, and denial-of-service assaults.

A complete ecosystem of network-connected devices, applications, and services, ranging from drones and autonomous cars to smart factories and mobile phones, will make more opportunities for hackers to get access to networks. There are security standards that each asset must be designed to meet. The network also gets more heterogeneous and harder to monitor and secure as the diversity of devices grows. New and unforeseen risks will emerge as the IoT continues to evolve and expand.

As a part of IoT, the introduction of mobile smartphones into our daily lives has been one of the biggest technological developments since the early 2010s. Our personal and professional lives are increasingly merging, particularly with the millennial and Gen-Z generations.

Data transfer from mobile and portable devices to the cloud can circumvent perimeter security. Once primarily targeting personal computers, cyberattacks are now targeting mobile devices and apps. While mobile devices' attack surfaces are expanding rapidly, security flaws are frequently disregarded, leaving sensitive data exposed.

The increasing sophistication and targeting of cyberattacks have made mobile security an increasingly pressing concern. This increases the danger of breaches and extortion for businesses and customers.

Particularly in the event of location-based emergencies, secure mobile applications can offer multimodal communications via SMS text, audio, mobile apps, and digital signs during an emergency. During such situations, evacuation rostering (accounting for employees during an emergency) can also be automated via mobile applications.

Mobility has emerged as our preferred method of working, playing, and reacting to events around us. This can be attributed to a variety of factors, including the addition of improved cybersecurity measures to protect data and the smartphone's role as a conduit for situational awareness and targeted messaging.

Insider Threats

One of the most challenging issues facing businesses, organizations, and nations is the cyber insider threat. Such threats might use a combination of hardware and software technologies, as well as human behavioral factors, making detection, defense, and remediation typically complex. Many of the threat actors are tech-savvy, and their infiltration techniques are getting increasingly advanced.

One of the main difficulties facing chief information security officers is countering insider threats that can be deliberate from a disgruntled employee or accidental because of employee negligence. Although spoof or phishing attacks can affect anyone, negligent behavior is frequently the result of a lack of security awareness brought on by subpar security policies, patch updates, compliance, and training. A portable memory device, misplaced documents, or unintentional revelation of privileged information are just a few of the many potential sources of accidental insider risks. Additionally, employees who bring their own devices to work run a higher risk of unintentionally introducing malware and viruses from their smartphones into company networks.

Insider threats can negatively affect a company's ability to conduct business, result in large financial losses, and damage the company's brand. Although there are no foolproof ways to completely protect against insider threats, risk management is a sensible way to lessen the chance of a breach. The maintenance and monitoring of allowed access should be governed by security protocols.

To understand vulnerabilities to insider threats, it is important to be able to define and categorize the types. The Information Security Forum (ISF) provides a solid framework for describing the types of insider breaches:[3]

- ◆ **Malicious.** Malicious insider behavior combines a motive to harm with a decision to act inappropriately, for example, keeping and turning over sensitive proprietary information to a competitor after being terminated.
- ◆ **Negligent.** Negligent behavior can occur when people look for ways to avoid policies they feel impede their work. Although most have a general awareness of security risks and recognize the importance of compliance, their workarounds can be risky.
- ◆ **Accidental.** ISF members report that completely inadvertent breaches are more common than malicious ones.

The three categories of insider breaches are concerning because of the widespread availability of sensitive data that can be accessed with ease if dynamic policies and fine-grained data in use restrictions are not implemented. Employees no longer only work within company networks; the quantity and variety of client devices using services have increased. After completing particular projects, virtual teams are assembled, modified, and then dissolved. Employees may still possess project-related information even after a mission or project has ended. Furthermore, as business boundaries blur due to the increased usage of mobility, cloud computing, and external partner engagement, perimeter-based defenses are no longer sufficient.

The insider threat is a costly and common phenomenon that is frequently disregarded. The ramifications must be considered by businesses and the government. However, for a global business, whether they are hosted on-site or in the cloud, there are behavioral monitoring software solutions and programs built with more robust encryption. A primary concern must be safeguarding data and limiting its use.

The Cloud

The rapid adoption of cloud and hybrid cloud environments by the public and private sectors is pushing computing closer to the edge. Cloud and hybrid cloud storage is becoming increasingly popular for storing data from businesses and government agencies.

For cybersecurity, securing the cloud is a key step. Cloud and hybrid cloud computing is becoming used for storing data from businesses and government agencies. Markets for cloud computing are expected to be worth $947.3 billion by 2026. It's used by 96% of businesses. Individuals and businesses (84%) use the private cloud.[4] Cloud and hybrid cloud operations are becoming more appealing as security administrators' top concerns are now where and how data is secured.

Cybersecurity now faces additional difficulties as cloud-based services continue to become more prevalent. Misconfigured cloud settings, unsecured application interfaces (APIs), and data breaches resulting from cloud vulnerabilities are among the difficulties that organizations need to deal with. Cloud infrastructure is becoming more important for enterprises; thus, protecting these environments is essential to preventing data leaks and illegal access.

Because of the complexity of the systems, which need to be updated and protected from zero-day threats, the quick shift to the cloud introduces new kinds of security concerns. For this reason, integration needs to be at the forefront of security considerations for hybrid cloud setups. Integration calls for visibility into every aspect of the environment, including the public, private, and on-premise spaces, as well as the right instruments and regulations to guarantee uniform security standards.

To keep up with the demands for storage and analytics, industry and government are constructing bigger data repositories and pooling data centers. Approximately 328.77 million terabytes of data are created each day, which equates to about 120 zettabytes of data that will be generated this year, and 181 zettabytes of data that will be generated in 2025.[5]

It is an understatement to say that is a lot of information to store and track! For successful operations, business depends on having the capacity to safely store, organize, evaluate, distribute, and scale that data. Data storage on cloud or hybrid clouds, rather than on premises, is more than wise due to those functional needs.

Using cloud and hybrid clouds reduces costs, increases access control transparency, allows for the adoption of dynamic policies, and accelerates encryption (thereby lowering insider threats). Cloud security that is optimized reduces the possibility of hackers gaining critical access to data, as seen from the standpoint of a security administrator. As additional workloads go to the cloud, it is imperative to comprehend cloud security's nuances and maximize its advantages.

Cloud service providers can address security issues and safeguard data using a variety of techniques. Data protection is ensured via access management and authentication, which create access lists for various assets. Providing employees access to just the tools they require to perform their jobs is a staple of identity and access management. You can better protect important documents from malevolent insiders or hackers using credentials they have stolen by enforcing stringent access control.

Cloud service providers use security protocols to guard sensitive data while it's in transit. Masking, encryption, and virtual private networks are examples of data security techniques. Employees who work remotely can access company networks through virtual private networks (VPNs). Tablets and smartphones can be used remotely with VPNs. Firewalls safeguard both your end users and the perimeter of your network security. Firewalls protect cloud-stored apps from one another as well.

In a good cloud security practice, names and other identifying information are encrypted via data masking. By keeping sensitive information secret, this preserves the integrity of the data.

Critical Infrastructure Protection

The United States and other countries' vital infrastructure, including banking systems, chemical plants, water and electricity utilities, hospitals, communication networks, commercial and critical manufacturing, pipelines, shipping, dams, bridges, highways, and buildings, have been a prime target of cyber intrusions by adversarial nation-states and criminal hackers.

Since 2018, hackers and nation-state enemies have developed a greater understanding of industrial control systems, how to breach them, and how to use malware that has been turned into a cyber weapon. Gartner Inc. has predicted that by 2025, industrial facilities would be weaponized by cybersecurity threats, leading to casualties. According to the company, attacks resulting in fatalities can cost up to $50 billion annually.[6]

Recently, cyberattacks on global critical infrastructure were identified and highlighted as a major worry in the World Economic Forum (WEF) Global Risks Report. Attacks on vital infrastructure have proliferated across industries like energy, health care, and transportation, according to the WEF.[7]

The Russian invasion of Ukraine, which opened the door for the use of cyberweapons intended to take down vital infrastructure, served as an example of this worldwide threat. Russia has persistently attempted to target important Ukrainian infrastructures to support their war efforts, in line with the kinetic attacks. Ukraine's power infrastructure has already been successfully brought offline by

Russian cyberattacks, and the country's power grid is currently being attacked by both physical and cyber missiles.

The majority of the time, a skilled and organized Ukrainian cyber force has stopped the attacks. As the Colonial Pipeline attack and the SolarWinds hack have shown, Russian and Russian proxy cyber capabilities remain strong and constitute a threat not only to Ukrainian infrastructure but also to the West as a whole. The upcoming years will see them grow more intensely.

DHS's Cybersecurity and Infrastructure Security Agency (CISA) describes critical infrastructure as "the physical and cyber systems and assets that are so vital to the United States that their incapacity or destruction would have a debilitating impact on our physical or economic security or public health or safety."[8] The threats to critical infrastructure are growing and include phishing scams, bots, ransomware, and polymorphic malware that can change in form and avoid anti-malware protections.

DHS formed the CISA in November 2018 because of recognition of an urgent need for public and private sector cooperation. CISA's directives put a focus on the DHS mission of cyber preparedness and ensuring protection and resilience to critical infrastructure. DHS identified 16 sectors deemed critical because their assets, systems, and networks are considered vital to national economic security, safety, and public health:

- Chemical
- Commercial facilities
- Communications
- Critical manufacturing
- Dams
- Defense industrial base
- Emergency services
- Energy
- Financial services
- Food and agriculture
- Government facilities
- Health care and public health
- Information technology
- Nuclear reactors, materials, and waste

+ Transportation systems
+ Water and wastewater systems

DHS states on their website that cybersecurity threats to critical infrastructure "are one of the most significant strategic risks for the United States, threatening our national security, economic prosperity, and public health and safety."[9] DHS realized that there are serious risks from state threat actors to critical infrastructure and that a cyber-attack that might take down the whole American electrical grid and other vital infrastructure.

The private sector owns and regulates most of the essential infrastructure in the United States, which includes the defense, oil and gas, electric power grids, health care, utilities, communications, transportation, education, banking, and finance sectors. Democratic societies are by nature open and accessible, making protecting the key infrastructure an extremely challenging task.

The majority of vital infrastructures now function in an internet-accessible digital environment. The expanding number of networked sensors, along with trends of hardware and software integration, are changing the surface areas that hackers can target across all digital infrastructures. Any nation must face challenges with critical infrastructure and supply chains, but democratic societies, which are by definition transparent and approachable, face particular difficulties.

One crucial infrastructure that stands out as being especially susceptible is the energy sector. Power plants, utilities, nuclear power plants, and the electrical grid are all part of this energy ecosystem. It is a challenging task to defend vital information technology (IT), operational technology (OT), and industrial control systems (ICSs) against cybersecurity attacks. Every one of them has different access points, legacy systems, and emerging technologies in addition to distinct operating frameworks.

A change in these critical infrastructure risk environments has corresponded with a heightened DHS (CISA) collaboration with other agencies, and especially the private sector stakeholders who own most of the nation's vital infrastructure. DHS has had to step up assessing situational awareness, information sharing, and resilience research and development plans with these stakeholders to mitigate risk and protect critical infrastructure and key resources.

The following list represents a partial set of typical threats:[10]

◆ Terrorists and other nonstate actors seeking to destroy, incapacitate, or exploit critical infrastructures to threaten national security cause mass casualties, weaken the economy, and damage public morale and confidence.

◆ Criminal groups, attacking systems, using spam, phishing, and spyware/malware, identity theft, online fraud, and computer extortion for monetary gain.

◆ Business intelligence operators, including criminal organizations, conduct voluntary and on-demand industrial espionage.

◆ Individuals and groups "graze" the cyber world in search of victims, for a combination of thrill and monetary and training purposes.

◆ Botnet operators use compromised, remotely controlled systems to coordinate attacks and to distribute phishing schemes, spam, and malware attacks.

◆ Disgruntled insiders, poorly trained employees, incompetent contractors all create opportunities for outsiders to penetrate networks.

◆ National intelligence and psychological operations organizations use cyber tools for information gathering, regime destabilization, and as another way to further their strategic goals.

◆ Spammers use these methods to distribute unsolicited email with hidden or false information to sell products, conduct phishing schemes, distribute spyware or malware, or attack organizations (e.g., a denial of service).

◆ National and/or commercial organizations specialize in deploying spyware or malware against organizations or individuals for political and commercial purposes.

The Convergence Supply Chain for IT and OT

The cyber ecosystem is in a vulnerable situation right now because of cross-pollination. The boundaries are no longer clearly defined, and as cyber device capabilities and connections have increased tremendously, so too have sophisticated malware cyberattacks on supervisory control and data acquisition networks, IT and OT networks, and ICS. Given the convergence of various networks, the hazards have grown even greater. The expanding number of networked IT sensors connecting the devices, and the trend of integrating industrial hardware and software are changing the surface attack chances available to hackers in all digital infrastructures.

One pressing issue that calls for coordination is safeguarding the merger of IT and OT networks against cyberattacks. Each of them has its own operating structure, access points, and legacy systems, and they are all entangled in different rules and compliance requirements. Additionally, a persistent problem in IT, OT, and ISC cybersecurity is a lack of experienced workers with training.

From the standpoint of cyberthreats, things are becoming worse, and tired security operators in both IT and OT have nowhere to go. Artificial intelligence is currently being used by criminal hackers to scour IT networks for security holes and incorrectly configured codes.

In terms of hardware, hackers frequently look for open ports or hardware attached to industrial internet-connected systems. The convergence of the IT, OT, and ICS supply chains is the most concerning because it can leave attackers with several ports of entry and cross-pollination to gain access for breaches. This is especially true for older legacy OT systems that were not built to withstand cyberattacks. This is frequently accomplished via infiltrating networks with compromised or fake hardware and software, taking advantage of suppliers' lax security procedures, or using insider threats The intricate character of supply chain assaults is further compounded by the extended lag time between the discovery of a vulnerability and its exploitation.

Third-party risk and the visibility of their partners in the chain are particular concerns for the supply chain. There might be security gaps that are undisclosed and undetected until an attacker compromises these systems, in addition to known vulnerabilities that remain unpatched.

To address these expanding concerns, an IT/OT cybersecurity strategy must be both all-encompassing and flexible. The same security components that provide protection to physical security also provide protection to cybersecurity: layered vigilance, preparedness, and resilience.

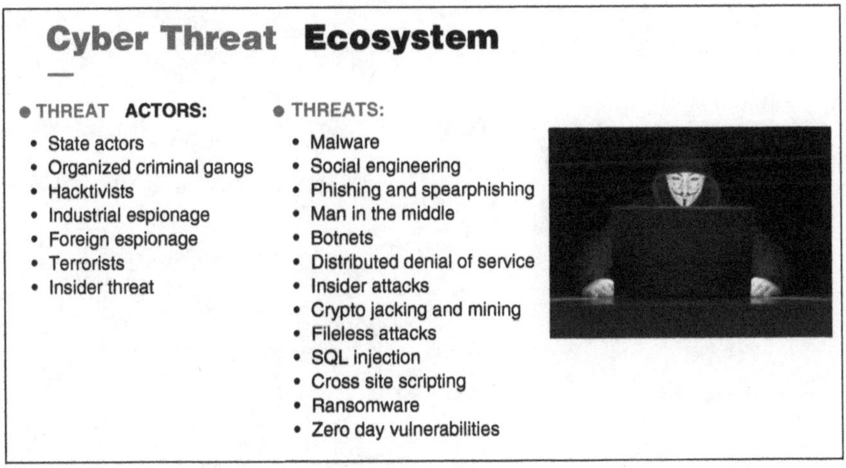

Cyber Threat **Ecosystem**
—

● THREAT **ACTORS:**

- State actors
- Organized criminal gangs
- Hacktivists
- Industrial espionage
- Foreign espionage
- Terrorists
- Insider threat

● THREATS:

- Malware
- Social engineering
- Phishing and spearphishing
- Man in the middle
- Botnets
- Distributed denial of service
- Insider attacks
- Crypto jacking and mining
- Fileless attacks
- SQL injection
- Cross site scripting
- Ransomware
- Zero day vulnerabilities

Figure 4.1   Cyber threat ecosystem.

In order to meet the problems, public and private collaboration is also needed for the exchange of threat intelligence, best practices, incident response, and cutting-edge technological solutions that can be used to lessen attacks on networks. This is a pathway not only for supply chain risk but also for any cyber threat. Figure 4.1 shows a summary overview of the cyber threat ecosystem.

CHAPTER 5

Cybersecurity and Digital Transformation

In the digital transformation of our Fourth Industrial Era, protecting user data in any cybersecurity approach needs to be dynamic and not static. Data has become more than a commodity; it is a driving force that determines how we live, earn, and function as a society.

Enterprises ought to be forward-thinking and embrace digital transformation and technology convergence. These trends are already having a considerable influence on how businesses function, and and although digital transformation can be a positive force, it needs to be guided by operational protocols, especially with concerns to cybersecurity.

Most of our vital critical infrastructures operate in a digital environment, including the health care, transportation, communications, financial, and energy industries. These cybersecurity areas need to be the focus and priority of risk management and cybersecurity framework for business:

- **Endpoint security.** Protecting remote access to a company's network.
- **Network security.** Protecting network from unwanted users, attacks, and intrusions.
- **Cloud security.** Protecting from unauthorized parties gaining access to an asset.
- **Mobile security.** Protection from fake and malicious apps.

- **Supply chain cyberattacks.** Protecting each component within the supply chain.
- **Data security and data privacy regulations.** Securing data and adhering to data and privacy standards.
- **Identity management.** Understanding the access every individual has to an organization.
- **Disaster recovery/business continuity planning.** Effective planning for the business to continue in the event of a breach.

For digital transformation, companies will need to make investments to bolster their cybersecurity defenses and provide employees with the skills necessary to tackle attacks. This entails conducting routine security audits, organizing incident response strategies, and elevating the security-first mindset.

In summary, the following is an overview of the threats to cybersecurity, along with some projections:

- Companies will place an even higher strategic priority on cybersecurity as the cost, complexity, and lethality of breaches keep rising.
- Significant operational and regulatory issues will arise with the introduction of emerging and fused technologies such as artificial intelligence (AI), 5G, IoT, and industrial IoT. To close gaps in widely used platforms, businesses and agencies will turn to automation and orchestration technologies like deep learning, AI, machine learning, and other analytical tools.
- Threat actors will use their resources to employ more sophisticated methods of identifying target vulnerabilities, automating their phishing attacks, and creating new, deceptive paths for malware infiltration. This is especially true for state-sponsored and criminal enterprises.
- Attacks using ransomware will become increasingly focused and persistent at a concerning rate. Soft targets for ransomware extortion are widely available, particularly in the manufacturing, finance, and health care sectors. Because many networks still have security holes that allow hackers to access data and because many of the affected firms are still paying

for ransomware, we should anticipate seeing more of these types of attacks.

◆ Cyberattacks against vital infrastructure are becoming more frequent and larger in scope. The attack surface has been further increased by digital connectivity brought about by the development of operational technology (OT) and the industrial internet of things. Because supply chains for IT, OT, and ICS in CI can cross-pollinate and provide attackers with several avenues of entry, they can be especially vulnerable. Additionally, older legacy OT systems were not built to withstand cyberattacks.

◆ Cybersecurity for supply chains is critical in the modern digital world. The complexity of security is in comprehending the interconnectedness of the supply chain landscape, identifying the most critical assets to safeguard, and skillfully putting methods for incident and breach mitigation and remediation into action.

◆ Enterprise technologies like AI, machine learning, and predictive analytics will be easier for chief information security officers (CISOs) to implement in order to increase the efficacy of threat analysis and mitigation. The necessity of the CISO position will increase as cybersecurity becomes a business survival and return on investment concern rather than just an IT one.

◆ The government's focus on cybersecurity issues will only increase in terms of strategy, funding, and procurement. The reorganization of government positions and resources is already indicative of this. The US Cyber Command, the Army Futures Command, the Department of Defense, the Navy, and the Air Force are already investing in new technology procurement and cybersecurity component training. Comparably, the Department of Homeland Security established the Cybersecurity Infrastructure Security Agency to concentrate on cybersecurity threats mainly affecting critical infrastructure on a civilian level. Seek increased funding to enable agencies to obtain the necessary cybersecurity technologies and knowledge.

◆ Keeping the supply chain safe will remain a top priority. Industry and government alike have identified supply chain security as a major concern. In an effort to protect the public and private supply chains from unjustified risk of sabotage, subversion of information and communications technology, or service design, integrity, manufacture, production, distribution, installation, operation, or maintenance, the White House recently issued a new executive order to address the threats to supply chains, especially in regard to protecting critical infrastructure.

- ◆ PPPs (public-private partnerships) are going to proliferate across the cybersecurity landscape. Open communication, sharing of risks, and cooperative research and development will spur creativity and make ideas easier to implement. PPPs will be viewed as positive news by the government and business community.

- ◆ The public and private sectors will continue to face significant difficulties due to a shortage of trained cybersecurity workers in the future. Automation won't solve the entire issue; it will only be a partial solution.

CHAPTER 6

Artificial Intelligence

What Is It?

We have been anxiously awaiting the advancement of artificial intelligence (AI) since director Stanley Kubrick gave us a peek at the HAL2000 computer that showcased AI's autonomous (but sinister) capacity to think independently in the classic film *2001: A Space Odyssey.*

AI emerges as a revolutionary force in an era of rapid technological growth, altering societal norms and reshaping industries. The trajectory of civilization will now be defined by exponential advances in technology that combine engineering, computer algorithms, and culture. It is not hyperbole to say that we are about to witness scientific and technical breakthroughs that will fundamentally alter the human situation. Surprisingly, the new age could alter how we relate to ourselves by means of machine learning (ML)-based computing and AI.

AI is defined by Gartner as "technology that appears to emulate human performance typically by learning, coming to its conclusions, appearing to understand complex content, engaging in natural dialogs with people, enhancing human cognitive performance or replacing people on execution of non-routine tasks."[1]

British mathematician Alan Turing pioneered AI. During World War II he proposed the concept of creating intelligent machines. To evaluate if a machine is capable of thinking or not, the Turing test, which he created in 1950, is still employed.

The phrase *artificial intelligence* was later used by John McCarthy, a professor at Dartmouth College, to describe this capacity at a conference in 1956, establishing the foundation for scholarly inquiry and the creation of "thinking machines."

AI systems aim to transcend human speed and constraints by mimicking human characteristics and computing abilities in a computer. ML and natural language processing, which are already commonplace in our daily lives, are components that contributed to the creation of AI. These days, AI is capable of comprehending, diagnosing, and resolving issues from both organized and unstructured data, sometimes even without the need for special programming. Large data sets are analyzed by AI systems in order to spot trends, anticipate outcomes, and automate decision-making.

AI is starting to become increasingly commonplace; it is no longer limited to science fiction films. In the next decade, we can expect to have computers capable of performing more than a quadrillion computations per second. We will also rely on the automation of knowledge work by intelligent computing software systems. AI and ML tools that will enhance cognitive performance will bolster our future computing in every vertical imagined. I like this quote by Microsoft's UK's chief envisioning officer Dave Choplin, who appropriately claimed that AI is "the most important technology that anybody on the planet is working on today."[2]

CHAPTER 7

Types of Artificial Intelligence

It is important to understand the different elements and subgroups associated with artificial intelligence (AI) to learn how it functions and what may be its potential applications.

Reactive AI, also known as narrow AI, is the most fundamental kind of AI. It is designed to produce a predictable result in response to input. Reactive robots are incapable of learning new behaviors or imagining the past or future; they always react to the same circumstances in the same way every time. Reactive AI is exemplified by Deep Blue, the renowned IBM chess machine. Google's AlphaGo is another example of a reactive machine.

Limited memory AI analyzes data or behaviors and creates experiential knowledge to learn from the past. In order to create predictions and carry out difficult categorization tasks, this kind of AI combines preprogrammed information with historical, observational data. It is currently the type of AI that is most commonly used today.

Theory of AI is something both aspired and feared. With AI, machines will be able to develop actual decision-making abilities that resemble those of humans. AI systems possessing theory of mind capabilities will have the capacity to recognize and retain emotions, subsequently modifying their actions in response to those feelings during social interactions. Those kinds of emotional recognition capabilities are still at the early stage of testing.

Self-aware AI is a step beyond the currently most sophisticated kind of AI theory. AI will resemble human consciousness when computers are able to recognize and feel both their own emotions and

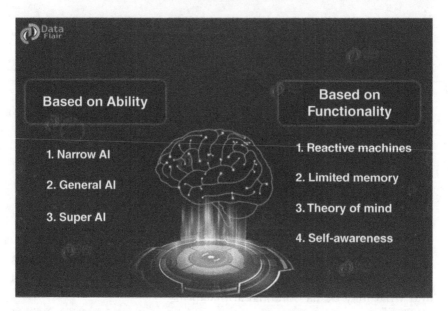

Figure 7.1   Types of AI.

those of others around them. AI of this kind will also have needs, wants, and emotions.

Figure 7.1 shows the various types of AI.

These definitions are useful because they provide guidance to AI concepts that provide the basis for future applications of AI.

CHAPTER 8

Some Subdomains of Artificial Intelligence

The following list describes some of the subdomains of artificial intelligence (AI). Later in the chapter, two of the enabling components of AI are introduced, followed by a list of common terms used in the discipline. The chapter concludes with a graphic showing how AI works.

- ◆ **Machine learning (ML).** ML is the science of making a computer behave without programming. ML allows a system to "learn" how to extract information from data on its own. It can be viewed as the quick automation of predictive analytics and frequently works in conjunction with AI. ML offers the quickest method for discovering new cyberattacks, deriving statistical conclusions, and delivering that data to endpoint protection platforms in the field of cybersecurity.

  ML trains a machine to draw conclusions and take actions based on prior knowledge. Without requiring the use of human experience, it finds patterns in historical data and analyzes it to deduce the meaning of individual data points and draw conclusions. Businesses may save time and make better decisions by using automation to evaluate data and draw conclusions.

- **Deep learning.** Deep learning is another ML technique. It teaches a machine how to classify, infer, and predict an outcome by processing inputs through layers.
- **Neural networks.** Human neural cells and neural networks operate according to comparable principles. These are a set of algorithms that process the data in a manner similar to that of the human brain, capturing the relationships among numerous underlying variables.
- **Natural language processing (NLP).** NLP is the study of how a machine can read, comprehend, and interpret language. A machine reacts appropriately after it determines what the user is trying to say.
- **Computer vision.** By dissecting an image and examining various aspects of the item, computer vision algorithms attempt to comprehend an image. In order to improve its output decision-making based on prior observations, this aids the machine's ability to classify and learn from a series of photos.
- **Cognitive computing.** By analyzing text, audio, images, and objects in a way that a human does and attempting to produce the intended result, cognitive computing algorithms attempt to emulate a human brain.

ML and NLP are two of the enabling components of AI that are commonly present in our daily lives. These days, AI does not need to be specially designed to comprehend, diagnose, and, in some situations, solve issues.

To understand AI, it is useful to be familiar with the most common terms used in the discipline:

- An *algorithm* is the process by which machines carry out tasks The steps are combined into equations because the machine is best at understanding numbers.
- *Artificial neural networks* are computer programs that mimic linked neural units and the interactions between neurons in the brain.
- *Cognitive science* and *AI* study how our brains process information and make decisions. Learning more about cognition is the primary objective.

- *Deep learning* is the application of a neural network made up of numerous layers and a large number of artificial neurons. Extensive and intricate data sets are ideal for deep learning.
- An *expert system* simulates a human expert's capacity for decision-making. Expert systems operate using "if-then" statements.

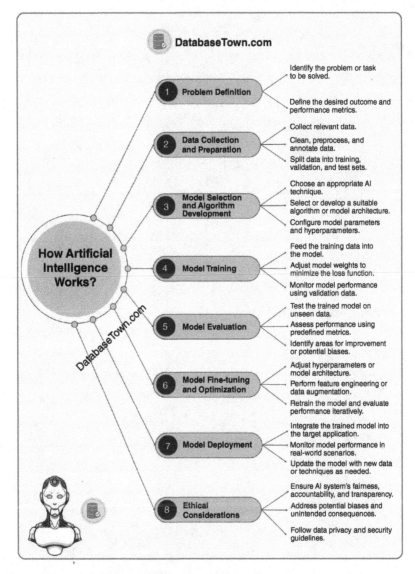

Figure 8.1   How artificial intelligence works.

Source: https://databasetown.com/how-artificial-intelligence-works/

Finally, the infographic in Figure 8.1 provides a good working diagram that shows how AI actually works.

Understanding the components of AI is integral to developing strategies and applications for industry uses and, of course, for cybersecurity.

CHAPTER 9

Big Data and Data Analytics

New paradigms for cybersecurity automation may emerge from artificial intelligence (AI) and machine learning (ML). They enable statistical conclusions to be made using predictive analytics, reducing the number of resources needed to mitigate hazards.

AI and ML have the potential to detect new assaults more quickly, make statistical inferences, and deliver that data to endpoint protection platforms in the context of cybersecurity. Intelligent algorithms and vast data sets are combined by AI and ML to evaluate, comprehend, and forecast future conditions. Large volumes of data are acquired from several sources, processed, analyzed, and structured in a format that the AI algorithms can understand in order to provide the kind of accurate predictions that AI systems need to make.

Basically, large-scale pattern matching is what AI does. Contemporary AI is capable of image identification, natural language comprehension, writing patterns analysis, linking disparate data sets, spotting anomalies in patterns, planning, forecasting, and much more because of its advancements in pattern recognition.

Though machines can process vast amounts of data more quickly than people can, robots have trouble with anomalies—outliers that defy training data and might be obvious to humans. The finest AI applications, therefore, are laser-focused and fuse the power of ML with human thinking.

Intelligent systems and ML can benefit greatly from AI and ML. Drives that can self-encrypt and heal themselves are examples of automated network security systems that safeguard data and programs. The scanning of horizons and real-time reporting on deviations and anomalies from networks can be made possible by cognitive automation. Automated cybersecurity diagnostics and forensics analysis are part of this automation, as are the defense framework layers (firewalls, payload, endpoint, network, and antivirus).

Being proactive and regularly testing and updating cybersecurity skills is necessary to counter these machine-driven hacker attacks. Countermeasures include using AI and ML to identify and forecast anomalies linked to the database of hostile threat behavioral patterns. Another useful tactic to avoid or deceive any hacker attacks is to use adaptive data deception technology.

With AI comes data, some of it quite large and diverse. The term *big data* describes the vast, varied collections of data that are expanding at an exponential pace. Information volume, creation and collection velocity, and the range or depth of the data points covered are all included.

Big data includes the data governance of all types of information, such as social media, audio and video, unstructured text, spatial data, and 3D data. There are data points everywhere, originating from the surrounding sensor networks and serving as the foundation for both our personal and professional endeavors. Data collection, its organization, taxonomy, and the automated analytics (including predictive) surrounding it, will determine the decisions we make in life on what, why, and how.

A wealth of information is being produced by digital technologies, which are linked to intelligent systems backed by ML and AI algorithms. This information is only waiting to be accessed and used. Data is now more than just a commodity; organizations can use data to gain valuable insights about their constituents, clients, and business processes, which empowers decision-makers to make well-informed, strategic business decisions.

Data analytics is not a subdomain of AI, but it does benefit from the capabilities of AI and ML. There are two general classifications of data: structured and unstructured. Structured data is very well organized and simple to understand; it is generally classified as quantitative data. The programming language used to manage structured data is called structured query language, or SQL. Business users may input, find, and modify structured data fast by using a relational (SQL) database.

Conventional data tools and methodologies are insufficient for processing and analyzing unstructured data, which is sometimes referred to as qualitative data. Structured data can be defined and found through searches. Dates and phone numbers are among the information contained in this. Everything else, such as emails, movies, podcasts, social media posts, and images, is considered unstructured data because it is more challenging to search or categorize. Unstructured data makes up the majority of data in the world.

With its intricate web of text, video, image, and other data forms, most digital data is unstructured. There is an estimated 80%–90% unstructured data volume in the world today, and it is rising faster than ever before. It will take sophisticated data analytic tools to even begin to make sense of this volume of data.

Unstructured data works best in non-relational databases because it lacks a predetermined data model. Using data lakes to store unstructured data in its unprocessed state is an additional method of managing it.

Businesses can employ data analytics to extract value from such data and close the knowledge gap, providing them with the means to identify patterns, consumer preferences, demographics, trade flow, transportation, and other associated factors. Reengineered for decision-making, the process is called *optimization*. These techniques are also beneficial to a number of other areas, such as financial services, health care, and customer service, where they may be used to detect caller trends, identify potential fraud, and proactively alert borrowers who are about to fall behind on their payments. Given that data analytics can boost output, effectiveness, decision-making, and new business ventures, agencies and companies cannot afford to overlook its importance.

Cybersecurity Ventures predicts that by 2025, 200 zettabytes of data will be stored worldwide. This covers information kept on utility infrastructures, private and public cloud data centers, personal computers, and IT infrastructures. By 2025, 200 zettabytes of data will be stored worldwide.[1]

The former CEO of Google, Eric Schmidt, claims that we generate more data every other day than we did from the dawn of humanity until 2003 put together. As such, data management, organization, and analysis are more crucial than ever.[2]

With limitless data sets containing different information, applied data analytics has a bright future. Large data sets with high volume, high velocity, and high variety necessitate creative, economical methods of information processing and will be required to improve understanding and decision-making. The application of data analytics will be aided by technological R&D advancements such as "machine thinking," which will enable linked devices on the Internet of Things to communicate with and learn from one another. These intelligent gadgets will enhance our knowledge and identify us through biometric authentications.

Data analytics is a science that is ingrained in the conversations and exchanges we have every day. The capabilities to organize, manage, and analyze growing amounts of data are more important than ever for our preparedness and economic prosperity.

CHAPTER 10

Generative Artificial Intelligence

The most popular type of artificial intelligence (AI) discussed in the media nowadays in generative AI. It is another subfield of AI. The term *generative AI* refers to a class of AI technology that broadly defines machine learning systems.

Generative AI is concerned with creating new data—such as text, pictures, videos—based on preexisting data. It involves devices and algorithms that learn from the massive volume of data they are provided, enabling them to continuously get better.

Though generative AI is not new—it has been around for many years—it is now much more user-friendly, accessible, and capable. Generative AI systems are now capable of processing, modifying, and producing text, including large language models (LLMs). These models may produce many textual styles that resemble content written by humans. Teaching an LLM to create new material requires feeding it a lot of information, such books, articles, and web pages. This enables the LLM to understand word patterns and connections.

The introduction of OpenAI's ChatGPT and DALL-E models, which gave consumers access to usable AI tools, has significantly contributed to the explosive rise in popularity of generative AI in recent years. Since then, in an effort to take advantage of the technology's quick adoption, major tech firms including Google, Microsoft, Amazon, and Meta have introduced their own generative AI tools.

An LLM is "trained" on copious amounts of textual material, usually downloaded from the internet, in order to make this possible. This could encompass websites and other open source materials like books, articles, and social media posts, depending on the LLM. The LLM's model may contain erroneous content because the training procedure involves so much data that it is impossible to filter it all.

The performance of LLMs is closely correlated with the quality of the data they consume, as they are voracious eaters of information. The ability of IT to rationalize enormous data estates, liberate mountains of unstructured data, and set up risk-mitigating controls is now critical to achieving enterprise generative AI adoption goals. Copyright problems brought up by generative AI are currently being looked into by the US Copyright Office. Facts and policy opinions about copyright law and policy will be gathered for this project and later analyzed.

Generative AI was initially made popular by ChatGPT, an AI chatbot. In a chat window that mimics human communication, the user can ask the bot for assistance with a range of tasks, including writing essays, emails, code, and other types of writing. It discovers correlations between words from this enormous corpus of material, and it may suggest words to read when prompted.

With the use of digital tools to generate code in response to incomplete code inputs or natural language prompts, developers can write code more quickly and frequently with the help of generative AI-assisted coding.

According to Gartner Research, the percentage of professional developers using AI-powered coding tools will increase from less than 10% in September 2023 to 70% by 2027. Additionally, 80% of businesses will have included AI-augmented testing technologies in their software engineering toolkit by three years.[1]

Gartner provided a good outline on the capabilities of generative AI for coding:[2]

◆ Generative AI code generation tools like GitHub Copilot, Amazon CodeWhisperer, and Google Codey are good choices for almost any enterprise seeking AI-enabled code generation tools.

◆ The use of non-enterprise LLM offerings, such as ChatGPT and Google Bard, by contrast, requires a number of trade-offs that many enterprises will find unacceptable. For example, your prompts and code may be included in future updates to the vendor products, which could put you in breach of data privacy regulations and leak critical intellectual property.

♦ Use plug-in coding assistants powered by machine learning to offer predictions of what single or multiline code fragments might come next, speeding the build.

♦ Interact with code assistants in an exploratory, conversational manner to help turn a vague idea into a program.

The foundation of original ChatGPT was a machine-learning model with 175 billion parameters that was trained on billions of web pages of text. The most recent version is bigger and accesses more data inputs.

Companies are rushing to release programs like GPT-3 that can write remarkably comprehensible articles and even computer code, because LLMs are one of the hottest areas of AI research right now. A group of AI forecasters, however, sees an issue approaching: we may run out of data to train them with.[3]

Texts from books, news articles, research papers, and Wikipedia are used to train language models. To make these models more accurate and adaptable, it has become common practice to train them on an increasing amount of data in recent years.

The problem lies in the fact that the kinds of data commonly used to train language models are limited and may run out.[4] The problem is that, in order to create models with ever-higher capacities, researchers must locate an increasing number of texts for training.

Industry Competing in Developing Generative AI

The most recent AI innovation from Google, the Gemini 1.5 Pro, performs 87% better on benchmarks than its predecessors, providing a major upgrade. With a remarkable accuracy of up to 10M tokens and a 100% recall for up to 530k tokens, it is an excellent choice for processing massive amounts of data. Tokenization splits text into smaller pieces that are easier for machines to read and understand.

Text, photos, videos, audio, and code can all be handled by the model with ease thanks to its sophisticated mixture-of-experts architecture and multimodal features. Additionally, Google has placed a strong emphasis on ethical deployment and safety, making sure that

Gemini 1.5 Pro raises the bar for responsible AI development. This model is a significant advancement in AI's capacity to comprehend intricate situations and carry out a variety of duties.

With the help of text descriptions, OpenAI has developed a state-of-the-art generative AI model called Sora. With the use of an intricate diffusion and transformer architecture, Sora is able to create intricate scenarios with several characters and movements, animate still photos, and fill in any gaps in recordings. It works with a range of video genres, up to one minute in length, including photorealistic and animated.

Apple plans to introduce an AI-powered coding assistant in Xcode, thereby entering the AI-assisted coding space and taking aim at Microsoft's GitHub Copilot. By automating processes like code completion and prediction and even translating code between languages, this technology seeks to increase developer efficiency. As part of a larger initiative to include AI into all of its products, Apple intends to include it in the upcoming significant releases for iOS, iPadOS, and macOS.

This program, designed to increase software development efficiency and make advancements in the field of generative AI, is an indication of Apple's efforts to expedite the coding and app testing process.[5]

Optimizing the Supply Chain

AI presents itself as a game-changer for optimizing supply chain processes and to boost productivity. Enterprises may attain scalability, agility, and competitiveness by leveraging AI-powered forecasting, optimization, and automation capabilities.

Specifically, AI can assist the supply chain challenges for business by doing the following:[6]

- ◆ **Predictive analytics.** AI algorithms can analyze historical data to forecast demand, identify trends, and anticipate supply chain disruptions, enabling businesses to proactively address issues before they occur.
- ◆ **Optimization.** AI-powered optimization algorithms can streamline supply chain processes, such as inventory management,

transportation routing, and warehouse operations, maximizing efficiency and reducing costs.

♦ **Automation.** AI-driven automation tools can automate repetitive tasks in the supply chain, such as order processing, inventory tracking, and demand forecasting, freeing up human resources for more strategic activities.

♦ **Real-time visibility.** AI-powered analytics platforms provide real-time visibility into supply chain operations, enabling businesses to monitor performance, identify bottlenecks, and make informed decisions in response to changing conditions.

Applications of AI in Supply Chain Management for Business Scalability

Let's explore some practical applications of AI in supply chain management for achieving business scalability:

♦ **Demand forecasting.** AI algorithms can analyze historical sales data, market trends, and external factors to forecast future demand more accurately, enabling businesses to optimize inventory levels and production schedules.

♦ **Inventory optimization.** AI-driven inventory management systems can analyze demand patterns, lead times, and supplier performance to optimize inventory levels and reduce carrying costs while ensuring product availability.

♦ **Supplier management.** AI-powered supplier management platforms can assess supplier performance, detect potential risks, and recommend strategies for optimizing supplier relationships, ensuring a reliable and resilient supply chain.

♦ **Transportation optimization.** AI algorithms can optimize transportation routes, modes, and schedules to minimize costs, reduce transit times, and improve delivery reliability, enhancing overall supply chain efficiency.

♦ **Warehouse automation.** AI-driven warehouse management systems can automate tasks such as order picking, packing, and inventory replenishment, increasing throughput and reducing labor costs.

Mind-Blowing Generative AI Statistics

Generative AI is changing the landscape from coding to analytics. The use of data analytics has been traditionally restricted to professionals in the industry due to its high learning curve and need for advanced equipment. Automation and intuitive interfaces that require little to no technical expertise are how AI is rewriting this story. Because of this, relevant insights can be gained from data even by those with little experience in analysis.

Generative AI has already affected industry and future planning. I recommend that you peruse Bernard Marr's "10 Mind-Blowing Generative AI Stats Everyone Should Know About," which provides insights into the near future on the potential of generative AI:[7] Thanks to AI and machine learning, the digital ecosystem's networked computing components will be equipped with a wealth of new features. Every industry will be affected by this convergence of technologies. AI has the potential to significantly transform both the economy and cognitive capacities. AI-enabled computers are made to automate tasks like learning, planning, speech recognition, and problem-solving. By using data to prioritize and act, these technologies can facilitate more effective decision-making, particularly in bigger networks with numerous users and factors. AI-powered computers are now being developed for a variety of fundamental tasks, such as speech recognition, learning and planning, and problem-solving.

AI-augmented automation is already being used by several businesses to increase efficiency. Businesses are already using robotic process automation (RPA), a type of AI, to cut down on manual labor and help prevent human mistakes in routine tasks. Through the use of technology for routine, repetitive tasks, RPA improves service operations and frees up human talent for more difficult, higher-level problems. It is scalable and adaptable to performance requirements.

In the private sector, RPA is commonly used in contact centers, medical coding, insurance enrollment and billing, and claim processing. Chatbots, another automated type of bot, are used to automate manual phone, message, social networking, and other tasks. Along with RPA, these bots are also becoming more and more common in service platforms because they reduce costs and offer a better user experience.

Like RPA, generative AI has many functions that can increase efficiencies and reduce workloads. And it is already being adopted by organizations for customer relations management, report writing, and other administrative and creative tasks.

CHAPTER 11

The State of Artificial Intelligence and Smart Cybersecurity

Some Insights and Statistics

Artificial intelligence (AI) has a lot to offer cybersecurity in new capabilities and in the perspective of significantly augmenting defensive operations in threat environments. Everything anyone does online is influenced by the threat horizon. Therefore, a company or individual needs to know what is in your system and who might be acting strangely.

In a world where sensors and algorithms are convergent, automated cybersecurity solutions for threat detection, information assurance, and resilience may serve as the binding agents that enable enterprises to leverage emerging technology to the fullest extent possible while maintaining operational security. With on-premises systems, cloud computing, and edge computing, the total IT perimeter for many businesses and institutions is now more complicated and distributed, calling for improved threat detection, analysis, and incident response as well as increased visibility. This is the core component of smart cybersecurity.

Cyber-threat detection, filtration, neutralization, and remediation are all made possible by smart cybersecurity, which has great promise. Moreover, predictive and generative AI algorithms have the potential to leverage predictive models more efficiently in cybersecurity, leading to enhanced security data and superior results.

By examining user behavior and network patterns, behavioral analysis and anomaly detection can spot abnormalities early on. Using previous patterns, machine learning (ML) models and their powered predictive analysis enable firms to anticipate and get ready for new dangers. Smart cybersecurity will be designed to maintain a proactive defense posture by staying ahead of developing hazards.

AI and ML for Analytics

AI and ML computing systems are in the initial stages of becoming a primary requirement for cyber operations. Although AI is the more general idea of building intelligent computers that can mimic human behavior and carry out tasks that usually require human intelligence, ML refers to a computer system's capacity to learn from experience and get better without being explicitly programmed.

In today's hyperconnected digital world, *security operators need to be aware of everything* that is happening on your system and have the ability to spot anomalies—like malware or misconfigurations—quickly to prevent breaches.

AI technologies *offer a quicker way to recognize and prevent cyber threats*. These dangers include malware that is getting more advanced and dangerous, ransomware, and social engineering.

This tech trend has ramifications for cybersecurity. To put it plainly, *AI strengthens cybersecurity in our interconnected environment by acting as a catalyst and facilitator*. Anything that is linked must be robust and safe. That includes all sectors and verticals of the world economy.

Numerous cybersecurity firms are creating and improving AI-powered platforms that track network activity in real time by scanning files and data for anomalous or malicious credential use, unauthorized connections, unauthorized communication attempts, brute force login attempts, anomalous data movement, and data exfiltration. Businesses will be able to use this to protect against anomalies and make conclusions based on statistics before they are reported and fixed.

In fact, as shown in Figure 11.1, by 2030, the spending on AI for cybersecurity is estimated to be almost $134 billion.

AI Cybersecurity Insights

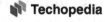 **Techopedia**

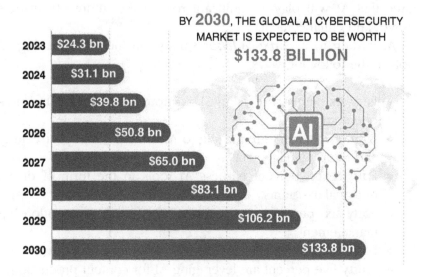

BY **2030**, THE GLOBAL AI CYBERSECURITY MARKET IS EXPECTED TO BE WORTH **$133.8 BILLION**

2023	$24.3 bn
2024	$31.1 bn
2025	$39.8 bn
2026	$50.8 bn
2027	$65.0 bn
2028	$83.1 bn
2029	$106.2 bn
2030	$133.8 bn

Figure 11.1   Project spending on AI by 2030.

Source: Napitu, Amanda (2024, January 17). 150+ artificial intelligence statistics you need to know in 2024 – who is using it & how? Techopedia. https://www.techopedia.com/artificial-intelligence-statistics

To summarize the state of AI and cybersecurity, the compiled statistics by CompTIA tell a good story of the uses and progress. Top AI statistics according to the CompTIA IT Industry Outlook 2024 report:[1]

♦ Twenty-two percent of firms are aggressively pursuing the integration of AI across a wide variety of technology products and business workflows.
♦ Thirty-three percent of firms are engaging in limited implementation of AI.
♦ Forty-five percent of firms are still in the exploration phase.

Hesitation in adoption may stem from challenges like the cost of upgrading applications, the cost of building out infrastructure, or the need to fully understand the data needed to properly train AI.

The State of AI in Business

Although some businesses are eager to adopt AI, and others are still exploring how the technology can benefit their organization, most agree that AI will play a significant role in the future of business growth and enhancement.

According to a *Forbes Advisor* survey, businesses are using AI tools in the following ways:[2]

- Fifty-six percent are using AI to improve and perfect business operations.
- Fifty-one percent are turning to AI to help with cybersecurity and fraud management.
- Forty-seven percent harness AI tools in the form of digital personal assistants.
- Forty-six percent are using AI for customer relationship management.
- Forty percent are turning to AI for inventory management.
- Thirty-five percent are leveraging AI for content production.
- Thirty-three percent are using AI for product recommendations.
- Thirty percent are turning to AI for accounting assistance and supply chain operations.
- Twenty-six percent harness AI for recruitment and talent sourcing.
- Twenty-four percent are using AI for audience segmentation.

Overall, there is a widespread adoption of AI in business.[3] But companies aren't using it for world domination but rather to automate processes, enhance customer service and personalization, increase output, and analyze data. Overall, businesses are trying to obtain a competitive advantage.

AI PRIORITIES AND PLANS

Creating a competitive advantage is good business practice. But jumping into AI isn't just an easy fix. BuiltIn reports the following risks and urges companies to prioritize the following when it comes to AI:[4]

- Automation-spurred job loss
- Deepfakes
- Privacy violations
- Algorithm bias caused by bad data
- Socioeconomic inequality
- Market volatility
- Weapons automatization
- Uncontrollable self-aware AI

AI MARKET STATISTICS

It's clear that AI is enabling many business segments across industries worldwide to grow. The potential for the AI market is untapped at this point. It's hard to predict quantifiable market growth when AI tools, technologies, and use cases are still being created.

Here's what we know:

- *Forbes* cites the global AI market size as valued at $136.55 billion in 2022.[5]
- NextMSC posts the global AI market size as worth approximately $207.9 billion in 2023.[6]

Here's what we expect:

- Similar web reports project the global AI market size is expected to be worth $407 billion by 2027.[7] That's a compound annual growth rate of 36.2% from 2022.
- Precedence Research projects the US AI market size to reach about $594 billion by 2032.[8] That's a compound annual growth rate of 19% from 2023.

AI GROWTH

We've been talking about AI growth in terms of metrics and the global economy. But the growth of new technology can be measured by more than numbers. The impact AI has already had on the way we live and work, combined with its potential to further revolutionize our lives, is arguably more important. From self-driving cars to health and wellness tools and navigation applications, how AI grows from here begs a few questions to consider:

- How do we minimize unintended bias?
- How do we ensure transparency?
- How do we protect privacy?

Although plenty of discussion surrounds these core questions, there isn't an easy, correct answer. It's essential that as AI continues to grow and evolve, we continue to invest in research and development with these issues in mind. Of equal importance is the careful consideration of policies and regulations that promote the responsible and ethical use of AI, similar to the California Consumer Privacy Act in the United States and the General Data Protection Regulation in Europe.

OBSTACLES TO AI ADOPTION
Despite the snowballing adoption rates of AI and advancements in AI technology, there are some barriers that are preventing organizations from implementing AI. CompTIA has identified the top obstacles to AI adoption:[9]

- Lack of skilled individuals and hiring shortages
- Unclear return on investment metrics
- Complexity of AI systems
- Lack of governance
- Fear of job replacement

But understanding your clients' specific needs and goals can help you customize your AI strategy and enhance your services.
Consider the following questions:

- Where are the two or three spaces that you could add the most value to your customers?
- What differentiating capabilities can you build that only you can bring to your customers using AI?
- Who are you going to turn away from using AI?
- What do you hope to achieve by implementing AI? Are you looking to improve efficiency, reduce costs, or enhance the customer experience?

A good overview of the requirements and paths for developing an AI strategy—use cases, challenges, and best practices—was summarized by the cybersecurity training organization, CompTIA (https://connect.comptia.org/blog/developing-an-ai-strategy-use-cases-challenges-and-best-practices).

BENEFITS OF AI ADOPTION

Adopting AI can have positive benefits for business, including (but not limited to) the following:

- Reduced operational time
- Greater business insight
- Reduced human error
- Automation of rote tasks
- Enhanced productivity
- Better customer service

IMPACT OF AI ON JOBS AND THE EMPLOYMENT MARKET

Many have expressed concern for their job status with the impending growth of AI and ML:

- IBM reports that 30% of IT professionals say their colleagues are using AI and automation tools to save time.[10]
- eMarketer says that 69% of executives believe AI will lead to the emergence of new jobs.[11]

Despite the negative perceptions:

- AI technology is expected to create 12 million more jobs than it is expected to replace.[12]
- Jobs are anticipated to be in high demand, with 97 million specialists needed in the AI industry by 2025.
- More than $1 in $4 invested in American start-ups in 2023 went to an AI-related company.[13]

A Simplilearn article explains the top AI applications being used across industry sectors:

eCommerce
- Personalized shopping apps
- AI-powered assistants
- Fraud prevention

Education
- Automated administrative tasks
- Creating smart content
- Voice assistants
- Personalized learning

Health care
- Detect diseases
- Analyze chronic conditions
- Discovery of new drugs

Agriculture
- Identify deficiencies in soil
- Analyze weed growth patterns
- Harvest crops at a higher volume and a quicker rate

Marketing
- Targeted and personalized ads
- Performance metrics
- Campaign optimization

ML AND AI STATS

Taking part in ML, AI, and big data is at the top of the priority list for many organizations. According to IBM:[14]

- Thirty-four percent of companies currently use AI, and an additional 42% are exploring AI.
- Thirty-five percent of organizations are training and reskilling their teams to use new AI and automation tools.

The entertainment giant Netflix is also known for its use of ML and AI software in content recommendations, which the company reports as saving $1 billion per year.

VOICE SEARCH AND AI STATS

With the prevalence of technologies such as Amazon's Alexa and Apple's Siri picking up speed, voice search has certainly taken its place in the emerging tech space. According to Tech Jury:[15]

- Ninety-seven percent of mobile users are using AI-powered voice assistants.
- More than 4 billion devices already work on AI-powered voice assistants.
- Forty percent of people use the voice search function at least once every day.

VIRTUAL ASSISTANTS

Disruptions in the workplace have given virtual assistants a boost as workers find more efficient ways to work in a decentralized environment:

- Fifty percent of knowledge workers will use a virtual assistant by 2025, according to Gartner.[16]
- GoGlobe reports that 54% of users agree that virtual personal assistants make their lives easier.[17]

AI IN THE RETAIL INDUSTRY

Currently, the retail market is embracing the use of AI due to its ability to hyper personalize and make recommendations based on product selection:

- AI spending in the retail industry is expected to reach $20.05 billion by 2026, a compounded annual growth rate of 39% since 2019.
- Eighty percent of retail executives expect their companies to adopt AI-powered intelligent automation by 2027.
- Juniper Research reports a growth of 230% in ML spending between 2019 and 2023.

AI IN CUSTOMER SERVICE

AI certainly has been beneficial in the customer service realm. Semrush reports the following AI statistics:

- Eighty percent of marketers already had chatbots as part of their customer experience strategy.
- Forty percent of businesses say that customer experience is their top motivator for using AI.
- Chatbots responded to 85% of customer service interactions.

CHATBOTS AND AI FACTS AND FIGURES

Many companies are embracing AI to support their customer service, most notably when it comes to customer interactions via chatbots. BloggingWizard compiled the following chatbot statistics:[18]

- Twenty-three percent of customer service companies are currently using AI, according to Salesforce.
- IBM reports that using chatbots can reduce customer service costs by as much as 30%.
- Sixty-eight percent of users enjoy the speed at which chatbots answer, according to UserLike.

Despite these gains, chatbots don't come without challenges:

- Sixty percent of people still prefer to speak to a live customer service representative, according to UserLike.
- Sixty percent of people are also concerned that chatbots cannot accurately understand their queries, according to *Business Insider*.

AI IN MARKETING AND SALES

There are so many AI use cases when it comes to marketing. Semrush reports that marketing and sales prioritize AI and ML more than any other department:[19]

- Forty-eight percent of marketing leaders cite AI as making the most significant difference in how customers interact with them.

- Fifty-one percent of eCommerce companies use AI to provide a seamless experience.
- Sixty-four percent of business-to-business marketers consider AI to be valuable in their marketing strategy.

Marketers are using generative AI tools to create content for campaigns, social media, websites and more. Many say AI tools help generate ideas and provide inspiration.[20]

The CompTIA summary provides a good working outline that highlights the potential influences and applications of AI across industries and functions. That outline is likely to expand in users statistics and AI tool capabilities in the near future.

CHAPTER 12

How Artificial Intelligence Can Help Cybersecurity

In our interconnected ecosystem, artificial intelligence (AI), to put it simply, is a potent accelerator and enabler for cybersecurity. AI systems emulate human traits and computational capacities in a computer to surpass human speed and limitations. Regarding cybersecurity, AI machine learning (ML) offers the quickest means of detecting novel assaults, deriving statistical conclusions, and delivering that data to endpoint protection platforms. Real-time reports on deviations and abnormalities can be obtained from network monitoring and horizon scanning. It enables continuous diagnostic and forensics analysis for optimal cybersecurity as well as automatic updating of defense framework layers (firewalls, payload, endpoint, network, and antivirus).

The following is a breakdown of how AI functionally assists in cybersecurity.

AI algorithms can help make decisions more effectively by prioritizing and acting on data, especially in larger networks with more users and variables. The ability to locate, categorize, and combine data is a valuable ability for lowering cybersecurity threats.

Generative AI–powered technologies can also *enable developers to write secure code faster*. Thanks to new AI tools, platforms, and technologies, developers are already developing more secure code from the start; this also makes it simpler to repair issues as they come up.

AI and ML applications in *the fields of threat intelligence and network surveillance can be advantageous for cybersecurity.* Generative AI has the ability to extract pertinent data, optimal procedures, and suggested courses of action from the body of knowledge inside the security industry with remarkable speed. With this thorough background information, practitioners can promptly ascertain the type of attack and the appropriate course of action. This in and of itself can cut any bad actors' dwell time from days to mere minutes, which is a big advantage for cyber defenders.

Intelligent algorithms can be used to monitor abnormalities in the network, identify new threats without clear indicators, and take appropriate action. It can also be used to correlate data from silos in order to assess network risks and vulnerabilities and identify the kind of assaults that are occurring.

A key component of zero trust cybersecurity, *identity and access management may benefit from AI and ML* by cross-checking the accuracy of data across many distributed databases.

One common workflow component for a security operations center (SOC) is *security log management.* That includes log review, data interpretation, and operations like threat hunting. AI can aid in all those functions.

Even in the absence of explicit guidelines, *AI is able to recognize abnormalities and departures from the norm.* It can do so by monitoring network activities in real time by analyzing data and files to identify illicit connections, unwanted communication attempts, strange or malicious credential use, brute force login attempts, abnormal data transfer, and data exfiltration.

AI is also proactive. Conventional signature-based detection techniques are frequently reactive and find it difficult to stay up-to-date with the constantly changing cyber threat scenario. However, organizations may proactively discover suspicious patterns and behaviors that may indicate possible threats or compromises by using AI ML algorithms that have been trained on massive volumes of data. By making it possible to identify zero day or previously unidentified assaults, this method offers a significant edge in the field of cybersecurity.

The automation and orchestration of security with AI has the potential to completely transform cybersecurity operations. AI is capable of automating and coordinating a range of security processes, including incident response and vulnerability management, by using ML and advanced analytics. As a result, security procedures are carried out consistently and on time, increasing efficiency.

AI could establish optimal approaches to cybersecurity automation. AI makes it possible for predictive analytics to form statistical deductions that require fewer resources and distribute this data to endpoint protection platforms.

Researchers from the Computer Science and Artificial Intelligence Laboratory at MIT and the ML start-up PatternEx presented a paper that detailed the AI platform known as AI2, which continuously incorporates expert human input to predict cyberattacks with a significant improvement over current systems. (The term is derived from combining AI with "analyst intuition," according to the researchers.)

By reducing the frequency of false positives by a factor of five, the researchers demonstrated that AI2 can detect 85% of attacks, which is approximately three times better than previous benchmarks. Over a three-month period, millions of users created 3.6 billion data points, or "log lines," which were used to evaluate the system.[1]

AI systems can also use behavioral analysis to examine trends and actions in enormous volumes of data. This enables cyber defense providers to draw statistical conclusions and prevent anomalies before they are identified and addressed.

By decreasing noise, delivering priority warnings, using contextual data backed by proof, and performing automated analysis based on correlation indexes from cyber threat intelligence reports, AI also improves network monitoring and threat detection tools to support cybersecurity professionals.

Because insider threats frequently originate from people who have in-depth knowledge of an organization's systems, they can be difficult to discover. Businesses can leverage AI's ability to recognize behavioral patterns to identify user behavior anomalies that might otherwise be overlooked. The system might identify something for evaluation, for example, if an employee downloads a lot of data all of a sudden or accesses private material unrelated to their job.

AI can also be a guard against impersonators. A synthetic image of a person's likeness is called *deepfake technology.* Social engineering assaults are more likely when using deepfake technology.

Automation is essential in the field of cybersecurity, according to Art Coviello, a partner at Rally Ventures and the former chair of the company RSA. "There are too many things happening—too much data, too many attackers, too much of an attack surface to defend—that without those automated capabilities that you get with AI and ML, you don't have a prayer of being able to defend yourself," Coviello said.[2]

Applications and dangers have boundaries, just like any other technology. Though there are some error levels and the potential for false positives or false negatives when using AI to detect threats in a network, *cybersecurity solutions driven by AI undoubtedly offer a high degree of accuracy and performance.*

Automated and flexible network applications can be made possible with the use of AI and ML. Automation makes network monitoring and horizon scanning that can deliver real-time reports on deviations and anomalies.

AI threat-hunting systems can span clouds, data centers, office networks, and Internet of Things devices. It automatically updates the network, payload, endpoint, firewall, and antivirus software layers of the defense framework in addition to performing cybersecurity diagnostics and forensics analysis.

Automation and adaptive networks themselves can benefit from the integration of both AI and ML. Programs for self-encrypting disks can enable automated network security to safeguard vital infrastructure across all domains. Horizon scanning and network monitoring that can provide real-time reports on deviations and anomalies are made possible by automation. It makes cybersecurity diagnostic and forensics analysis, as well as the defense framework's layers of network, payload, endpoint, firewall, and antivirus software, automatically updated. By adding analytics to specialized data sources, it can also be used for threat vetting.

Security orchestration automation and response (SOAR) systems can also benefit from AI and ML by unifying orchestration methods, automation, incident management and collaboration, visualization, and reporting under a single interface. In addition, SOAR can help SOC staff locate and resolve prospective or ongoing threats by providing a speedier, more accurate method for managing the enormous volumes of data produced by cybersecurity systems.

For patch management and vulnerability evaluation, generative AI can assist in prioritizing vulnerabilities according to their business impact and recommending efficient patch management solutions by modeling attack scenarios. In addition to patch management, generative AI can also be used to prioritize risks and generate personalized suggestions for risk mitigation and threat response that can enhance both remediation and response.

For training, generative AI systems are being used by SOCs to automate routine documentation and triage chores. This frees up entry-level security analysts to focus more of their time on core skill development, composing answers, and conducting investigations. Technology can be another helpful tool in an analyst's toolbox; it can improve accuracy, serve as a knowledge base, and collect data rapidly and effectively.

For years, Secureworks, a company that manages its own SOC and offers SOC services and software to clients, has been using AI in various forms. The business employed a variety of technologies, from neural networks to other ML models and anomaly detection. These methods assisted Secureworks in gathering and sorting warnings, enabling analysts to concentrate on the most important ones first. The organization experienced a 50% decrease in analyst workload and an 80% decrease in alerts over the preceding 18 months, freeing up the analysts' time to work on more challenging cases and on assisting new clients.[3]

Menlo Ventures thinks that generative AI will make security training more dynamic, personalized, and entertaining for employees— better simulating dangers and scenarios found in the real world. For example, Immersive Labs simulates assaults and situations for their security team using generative AI. Using Slack or the internet, a security copilot guides riot staff members through interactive security awareness training. These kinds of tools, according to Menlo Ventures, will boost the efficacy of security training.[4]

Mitigating AI Threats

Mitigating threats is an important cog of AI for cybersecurity. A state of AI and security survey report of 2,486 information technology and security professionals, conducted by Google Cloud and the Cloud

Security Alliance released in 2024, found that 55% of businesses worldwide intend to adopt AI to enhance corporate cybersecurity. Additionally, according to the report, 19% of IT decision-makers believe that attack simulation and compliance violations would ultimately prove to be the most likely cybersecurity use cases in 2024, and 21% of them believe AI may assist them in developing security policies.

"The advent of AI in cybersecurity marks a transformative era in the realm of digital defense, bringing a blend of promising breakthroughs and intricate challenges," the researchers wrote in their survey. "AI has the potential to be a vital ally in bolstering security defenses, identifying emerging threats, and facilitating swift responses."[5]

Recently, the Social Security Administration was involved with a case in which a foreign chatbot pretended to be many SSA recipients to change the details of a direct deposit account. Luckily, they were able to discover and mitigate it.

According to the inspector general of the Social Security Administration,

> Artificial intelligence is rapidly becoming a primary driver of emerging technologies and is impacting society in ways the public and private sectors are just beginning to understand. According to the National Institutes of Justice, AI is becoming an important technology in fraud detection. Internet companies and financial institutions thwart fraud attempts by using large data sets to continuously train their fraud detection algorithms to predict and recognize anomalous patterns indicative of fraud. AI will be a powerful tool to support the federal government's ability to detect and prevent the fraudulent disbursement of taxpayers' dollars.[6]

Descriptive analytics provided by network surveillance and threat detection technologies can answer the question of "what happened?" in breach forensics; AI-enabled incident diagnosis analytics can answer the questions "why and how did it happen?" AI-powered software applications and platforms can examine past data sets to look back at change and abnormality indicators in the network activity in order to find the answers to those questions.

If an incident investigation reveals a system vulnerability (as opposed to malicious exploitation), predictive analytics may provide information on the implications. Once the reasons of an occurrence have been identified, prescriptive analytics can be used to respond to it by making recommendations for containing and permanently eliminating those causes. These recommendations can be implemented in a variety of ways, including the adoption of targeted measures, modified strategies, and new policies or procedures.

These days, supply chain processes are tracked, alerted, and assessed using cutting-edge technology like blockchain and AI. Vulnerability assessments and cybersecurity techniques can close operational gaps.

AI enhancements to systems for identification and access control, encryption, log management, data loss prevention, and security information and event management (SIEM) platforms can all aid in reducing cyber threats. Software and objects can be tracked via stenographic and watermark technologies, and visibility and predictive analytics can be obtained through AI and ML methods. Naturally, employee education and cyber hygiene are important, as are measures for zero trust and visibility into all parties participating in a supply chain.

AI technologies can be implemented to assist cyber threat analysts and tackle the issue of excessive data and information overload. Among these solutions are open source AI-powered data collection tools that compile information on particular online dangers or vulnerabilities.

Using natural language processing, *AI machines can assemble, summarize, or even author a report entirely on the material.* AI algorithms can help make decisions more effectively by prioritizing and acting on data, especially in larger networks with more users and variables. The ability to locate, categorize, and combine data is valuable for lowering cybersecurity threats. Importantly, it can help analysts more efficiently filter false positive incident alerts.

AI can also be of significant assistance to cybersecurity analysts in the preparation of reports on cyber threat intelligence. These analysts are already short-staffed and deal with thousands of attacks on their systems every day, and the quantity, sophistication, and speed of malware attacks only increase. There is an abundance of information resulting from this cyber reality that is difficult to gather, arrange, and evaluate.

AI systems are already being used by a wide range of commercial enterprises to generate financial reports, social media posts, legal filings, and news articles. Similar methods are also used by the cybersecurity sector to produce automated cyber threat intelligence reports. Reports on cyber threat intelligence offer the early warning signs and indicators required to monitor anomalous activity more effectively on a particular network and identify cyber threats.

Generative AI could revolutionize cybersecurity operations and products. Following the introduction of large language model-powered applications like ChatGPT, generative AI is being used in the lessons learned phase, where it can enhance internal communication by automating the production of incident response reports. Most important, defenses can be strengthened by reintegrating the reports into the model.

According to Bain & Company, generative AI's ability to detect and hunt threats will only get more dynamic and automated. Some of the benefits are depicted in the infographic shown in Figure 12.1.

AI can help write better code. With better code quality and efficiency, generative AI may help write secure code, enhance code analysis, produce tests, write documentation, and aid with many other developer security operations (DevSecOps) tasks. This ability to understand contextual information has the potential to usher in a new age in software development.

Among the many other DevSecOps-related jobs that may be completed with generative AI are debugging, creating tests, providing documentation, and identifying security flaws in existing code.

In conjunction with adaptive practices, security-aware corporate cultures, and security frameworks, AI also empowers enterprises to mount a formidable and proactive defense. A proactive cybersecurity policy that prioritizes AI-powered threat detection and quantum-resistant encryption will be necessary as we drive digital transformation in the face of rising dangers.

For creating an optimized cybersecurity risk management framework, businesses and organizations can use AI and ML to automate tasks like setting up security policies, keeping an eye on compliance, and identifying and responding to threats and vulnerabilities.

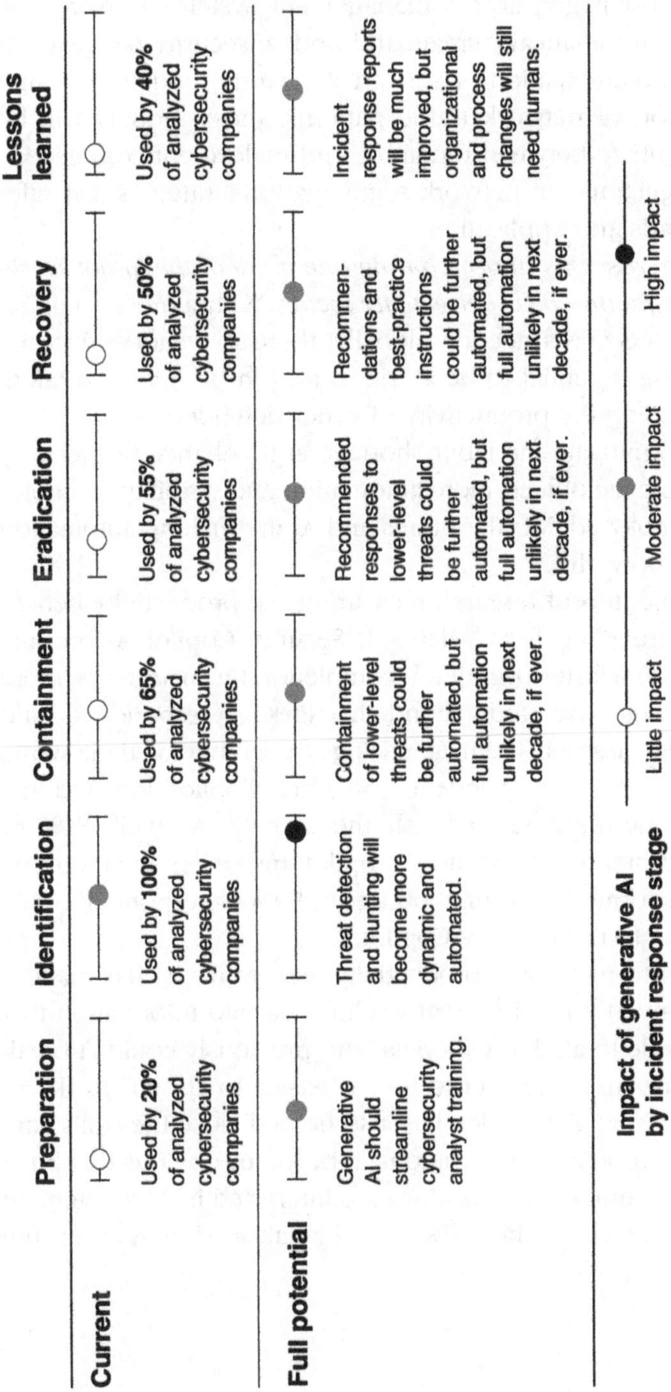

	Preparation	Identification	Containment	Eradication	Recovery	Lessons learned
Current	Used by **20%** of analyzed cybersecurity companies	Used by **100%** of analyzed cybersecurity companies	Used by **65%** of analyzed cybersecurity companies	Used by **55%** of analyzed cybersecurity companies	Used by **50%** of analyzed cybersecurity companies	Used by **40%** of analyzed cybersecurity companies
Full potential	Generative AI should streamline cybersecurity analyst training.	Threat detection and hunting will become more dynamic and automated.	Containment of lower-level threats could be further automated, but full automation unlikely in next decade, if ever.	Recommended responses to lower-level threats could be further automated, but full automation unlikely in next decade, if ever.	Recommendations and best-practice instructions could be further automated, but full automation unlikely in next decade, if ever.	Incident response reports will be much improved, but organizational and process changes will still need humans.

Impact of generative AI by incident response stage

Little impact — Moderate impact — High impact

Figure 12.1 Companies using Generative AI for cybersecurity.

Note: Percentages rounded; analysis is of cybersecurity companies that are using generative AI to enhance solutions.

Source: Bain & Company. https://www.bain.com/insights/generative-ai-and-cybersecurity-strengthening-both-defenses-and-threats-tech-report-2023/.

For example, privileged access management systems powered by ML are able to automatically create and update security policies that support the implementation of zero trust security models. Through the examination of network traffic patterns, these models will be able to differentiate between reputable and malevolent connections and offer suggestions on network segmentation strategies that safeguard workloads and applications.

AI can also assist us in overcoming one more of the major workforce obstacles facing the cybersecurity sector. With almost 4 million cybersecurity specialists needed globally, there is a shortage in the field. AI has the potential to be a critical tool in bridging the talent gap and increasing the productivity of cyber defenders.

In order to mitigate the labor shortage and enhance the security of remote employee offices, more automation and visibility technologies will be employed. ML algorithms and AI are making automation systems more powerful.

For example, recent research measuring the productivity benefit for "new in career" analysts, Microsoft Security Copilot AI product users showed 26% faster overall job completion times and 44% more correct responses. The study found that 86% of respondents said Security Copilot assisted them in raising the caliber of their work. According to 83% of respondents, Security Copilot lowered the amount of work required to finish the activity. As well, 86% of respondents claimed that Security Copilot increased their output. When they performed the same job again, 90% of respondents said they would like to use Security Copilot.[7]

In addition to increasing productivity, generative AI has made it possible to convert intricate threat intelligence into information that is understandable to all. Professionals who previously couldn't break into the cybersecurity field now find it easier to do so thanks to developing technologies, which has also helped close the skills gap.

Given those potential applications, it becomes obvious that businesses and government organizations are interested in AI to augment and partially automate the cybersecurity labor shortages in the workforce.

CHAPTER 13

The Other Side of the Artificial Intelligence Cyber Coin

Almost any technology can be put to good or bad use; it can be a double-edged sword. Though useful tools for cyber defense, artificial intelligence (AI) and machine learning (ML) potentially have drawbacks. Threat actors can employ them to do their bidding. The cybersecurity landscape is quickly changing, encompassing AI-powered malware, adversarial ML techniques, AI-enabled botnets, and intensified insider threats.

AI systems carry substantial risks for people, businesses, and even entire countries because they can be programmed or altered with malicious intent. Using AI and MI as tools, adversarial nations and malicious hackers are already able to identify and take advantage of flaws in threat detection models. They employ many techniques. That brings with it a new set of difficult challenges that businesses need to be ready to face. This chapter discusses some of those techniques.

Simply stated, the malicious application of AI can erode the benefits and put people and organizations at risk. This covers actions like identity theft, privacy and confidentiality breaches, algorithm manipulation, and hacking. Cybercriminals' use of AI presents an unprecedented risk to everyone's online safety. Businesses and consumers need to be on the lookout for, prioritize, and implement cybersecurity best practices in light of the rise in fraud attempts, AI-assisted SMS scams, and skillfully constructed phishing emails.

The use of AI is accelerating at an unprecedented rate, which fosters amazing innovation. Organizations must, however, make sure that they have visibility into and control over the entire AI stack being used. They must also thoroughly examine all associated risks, such as the use of malicious models, the exposure of training data, the use of sensitive data in training, and other vulnerabilities in AI that could be used by attackers.

Evolution of Threats in the Age of AI

Cyber threats were growing globally faster than cyber defensive capabilities even before AI arose and was used. Cyber resilience, or the capacity to control cybersecurity risk, is expanding along with the difference between the two.

General AI models can scan and analyze entire corporate computer systems, finding and taking advantage of the most common attack vectors and flaws when used maliciously. The speed and accuracy with which many modern algorithms can carry out these tasks is the main cause for concern.

Cyberattacks in the past required much manual investigation, labor-intensive planning, and patience. Threat actors, however, have used AI to their advantage and are now able to plan attacks with remarkable effectiveness. They can carry out more complex, difficult-to-detect attacks at scale because of this technological development. To further amplify the impact of their illicit activities, hackers can also alter ML algorithms to interfere with operations or compromise confidential data.

Optimization is the primary risk posed by the use of AI in cyberattacks. Because AI algorithms are always getting faster and more accurate, the information they can provide to criminals gets more precise and thorough over time, while the skills the criminals need to commit crimes themselves get less sophisticated.

Nation-state adversaries are already using those approaches. Threat actors are increasingly leveraging AI and large language models (LLMs) to speed up and improve the efficacy of their attacks. It has been disclosed by Microsoft and OpenAI that hackers are already using massive language models, such as ChatGPT, to hone and enhance their current cyberattacks. According to recently released research, Microsoft and OpenAI said they discovered and terminated OpenAI accounts associated with "five state-affiliated malicious actors" who were using ChatGPT and other AI technologies to launch cyberattacks. The accounts were linked to the following countries: China-affiliated Charcoal Typhoon (CHROMIUM) and Salmon Typhoon (SODIUM), Iran-affiliated Crimson Sandstorm (CURIUM), North Korea–affiliated Emerald Sleet (THALLIUM), and Russia-affiliated Forest Blizzard (STRONTIUM).[1]

According to Microsoft corporate vice president of security, compliance, identity, and management Vasu Jakkal, the organizations discovered that the threat actors used OpenAI's services to search for open source material, translate documents, seek for coding flaws, and perform other coding jobs.[2]

Cybercriminals are also taking advantage of vulnerabilities in the ecosystem of the growing networks of connected devices. They are using AI and ML tools to penetrate and investigate victim networks. Every connected device is a potential avenue for exploitation.

In an effort to trick or even compromise cyber defense systems and apps, criminals favored methods typically involve self-modifying malware and automated phishing attempts that imitate actual people. Then there is "drop malware," which includes worms, viruses, and ransomware that is intended to infiltrate and spread across networks, devices, or computer systems.

A favorite tactic of cybercriminals is to use business email compromise fraud schemes to trick victims by pretending to be a reliable person or entity. Attackers can produce emails using generative AI that closely resembles the vocabulary, style, and tone of the person or organization they are impersonating, making it harder to tell phony emails from real ones.

Malicious malware can employ AI to distribute itself by automating target selection, assessing compromised environments before launching further assault stages, and avoiding detection. Additionally, by using AI and ML, malicious software can be used to avoid detection, automate target selection, and investigate compromised environments prior to starting further phases of an assault.

As malicious actors continue to employ generative AI to standardize and update their strategies, methods, and processes, the threat they pose will only grow. Cyberattacks will become more sophisticated as a result of generative AI, increasing the possibility of ransomware-as-a-service, phishing, malware development, deepfakes, and the exposing of personally identifying information.

Specific threats aided by generative AI include malware strains that self-improve, developing variants to target a particular target using a special method, payload, and polymorphic code that evades detection by current security protocols. The most flexible cybersecurity operations will be the ones that maintain their lead.

Hackers will also use automated phishing applications via generative AI that imitate humans and can reach hundreds of thousands of targets. Cybercriminals are also gaining speed by using AI, which enables them to quickly modify their attacks in response to new security protocols. Malicious actors can quickly and readily modify a known attack code to make it sufficiently different from the original to evade detection thanks to generative AI.

Another kind of adversarial attack in the context of AI and ML models is AI poisoning. Here, harmful data is inserted into an AI or ML model's training data set. Aiming to provide biased predictions or degraded performance, the goal is to carefully modify the training data to affect the model's behavior. Attackers can compromise the model's dependability and integrity by introducing tainted data during training.

In the past, nation-state resources were needed to produce exploit programs, but modern crimeware gangs are becoming more capable than ever before with AI tools. The use of generative AI models is growing in popularity among fraudsters. Researchers from Netenrich have discovered a new platform called FraudGPT, which is promoted on several markets and the Telegram Channel. Nefarious features supported by the chatbot include the following:[3]

- ◆ Write malicious code.
- ◆ Create undetectable malware.
- ◆ Find non-VBV bins.
- ◆ Create phishing pages.
- ◆ Create hacking tools.
- ◆ Find groups, sites, and markets.
- ◆ Write scam pages/letters.
- ◆ Find leaks and vulnerabilities.

◆ Learn to code/hack.
◆ Find credible sites.

In fact, the results of Acronis's benchmarked cyber threats report for the second half of 2023 confirm the prowess of AI-directed phishing attacks. This was achieved by leveraging data collected from more than 1 million unique endpoints across 15 nations.

The Acronis report highlighted the alarming statistics.[4] The results disclosed show that AI-enhanced phishing affected more than 90% of enterprises and contributed to a 222% increase in email attacks in 2023 compared to the second half of 2022. Cybercriminals are leveraging malicious AI tools, including WormGPT, FraudGPT, DarkBERT, DarkBART, and ChaosGPT.

"There's a disturbing trend being recognized globally where bad actors continue to leverage ChatGPT and similar generative AI systems to increase cyberattack efficiency, create malicious code, and automate attacks," said Candid Wüest, Acronis VP of product management.[5]

The extraordinary embrace of generative AI by criminal hackers requires security techniques to change, and they must do so quickly. The rate at which new vulnerabilities are discovered and the speed at which attackers can use AI and ML to operationalize exploits are crucial factors for cyber defenders to address. Attackers are honing algorithms intended to steal privileged access credentials, personalizing phishing emails, and improving malware through the use of ChatGPT.

It is always beneficial to plan and consider potential future developments from a security perspective. Interactive AI is one of the most recent advances in AI technology. Although generative AI tools can write code, produce new content, carry out calculations, and have conversations similar to those of a person, interactive AI can be used for tasks like speech-to-text apps or geolocation and navigation, ushering in the next era of chatbots and digital assistants.

Shishir Singh, CTO of cybersecurity at BlackBerry notes,

It's been well documented that people with malicious intent are testing the waters, but over this year, we expect to see hackers get a much better handle on how to use ChatGPT successfully for nefarious purposes; whether as a tool to write better mutable malware or as an enabler to bolster their "skill-set." Both cyber pros and hackers will continue to look into how they can utilize it best. Time will tell who's more effective.[6]

According to a recent survey conducted by BlackBerry, 51% of IT decision-makers anticipate that ChatGPT will be involved in a successful cyberattack this year.[7]

AI-Generated Polymorphic Malware

If regular malware was not nefarious enough, hackers are now using AI to construct malware that can change its code at will, referred to as *polymorphic malware*. The malware self-modifies to trick or even undermine cyber defense systems and programs. Constantly changing malware is difficult to detect and eliminate.

Polymorphic malware leverages polymorphism to evade detection instead of optimizing its effectiveness. The idea behind polymorphic malware is that subsequent iterations of the infection might be able to evade detection by making small adjustments if a particular strain of malware is known for possessing specific traits.

This enables innumerable malicious files to perform the same function while appearing sufficiently unique to evade identification as malware. Polymorphic code can be found in many types of malwares, including adware, ransomware, rootkits, and key loggers.

Because polymorphic malware can get around two-factor authentication and other authentication security measures, it is already being exchanged more frequently by criminal hacking groups and might potentially become a severe problem in the future.

Using AI, nation-states and/or actors from criminal organizations can hide malware from users of widely downloaded programs. The malware is downloaded and then, after a set period of time, one or more pieces activate it.

Long-running attacks enable hackers to collect user data (identity management features, authentication procedure). Malicious AI (deep exploit) might aid intelligent malware that learns from both successful and unsuccessful attempts. Thus, clever malware can spread by finding and exploiting holes in systems, then launching new attacks to counter those holes in order to copy themselves. In addition, malicious AI has the ability to carry out stealth attacks by modifying its system to match the security environment of an organization.

The most susceptible are small and medium-sized enterprises, groups, and particularly medical facilities that lack the financial means to make large investments in defensive innovative cybersecurity technology like AI. Ransomware-enabled extortion by hackers requesting payment in cryptocurrency could grow.

More quickly than most commercial cybersecurity teams, criminal hackers have especially embraced generative AI, and they may use it for their gain. Attackers might easily send accurate, faultless, and relatable communications to a wide audience in multiple languages thanks to generative AI.

Moreover, by enabling the comparison of source code among various software versions and the discovery of both revealed and concealed flaws, generative AI has already sped up the hunt for vulnerabilities in open source software.

The cybersecurity company Tripwire provides a good summary of what traits are present in AI-driven cyberattacks:[8]

- ◆ **Automated target profiling.** AI simplifies attack research by effectively profiling targets through data scraping from public records, social media, and business websites. Data analytics and ML are used to do this.
- ◆ **Effective information gathering.** AI streamlines and expedites the reconnaissance phase, the initial active stage of an attack, by automating the process of searching for targets on several internet platforms.
- ◆ **Personalized attacks.** AI uses data analysis to produce highly accurate personalized phishing messages, which raises the possibility of successful deception.
- ◆ **Employee targeting.** AI finds important employees in businesses who have access to private data.
- ◆ **Reinforcement learning.** AI uses reinforcement learning to continuously improve and adapt in real time to attacks. It modifies strategies based on past encounters to remain adaptable, increase success rates, and outsmart security defenses.

The Employees, Risk of Using AI

An analysis of the risks and ways in which employees use generative AI was published in a report by Menlo Security on the effects of generative AI on security posture.[9] User attempts to enter personally identifiable information into generative AI websites accounted for 55% of data loss prevention events that occurred in the last 30 days. Confidential documentation trailed behind personally identifiable data, accounting for 40% of the efforts.

The report exposed security vulnerabilities related to the evolving field of generative AI. Although there was a 6% decline in copy-and-paste inputs, these attempts are still common. Moreover, an 80% rise in file upload attempts was observed. Because client lists and personally identifiable information can be supplied quickly and easily, these applications of generative AI present a cybersecurity risk.

The conflict between worker productivity and security has intensified with the emergence of generative AI. Although employees are drawn to generative AI due to its promise to increase productivity and efficiency, security teams are concerned that it could increase the surface area for assaults.

Ninety-two percent of security professionals are also concerned about generative AI security. Specifically, they are worried about employees using AI tools with sensitive company data (48%), training AI systems with harmful or inaccurate data (44%), and falling for phishing attempts with AI enhancements (42%).[10]

Fifty-seven percent of respondents claim that they are more productive and save time at work when they use generative AI solutions. Additionally, a little but noteworthy percentage of workers (22%) acknowledge knowing that they have broken workplace policies regarding the use of generative AI.

AI-Generated Deepfakes

The word *deepfake* refers to the underlying technology, deep learning algorithms, which may be used to produce fake material (including about real people) by self-learning using massive data sets.

Using text, image, and music as inputs, generative AI swiftly creates new content by using deep neural network ML algorithms. Then, in addition to photos, generative AI models can generate incredibly lifelike text, audio, and video output. Many deepfake AI-generated audio files are sufficiently lifelike that an attacker can use them to convincingly assume the identity of businesses, CEOs, and bank account information.

Although deepfakes can be produced in a variety of ways, the most popular approach uses deep neural networks with a face-swapping algorithm inside them. The foundation of the deepfake is a target video, which you will need to obtain initially, along with a selection of video clips featuring the subject of the deepfake.

The target video may be a scene from a Hollywood production, for instance, and the person whose films you wish to include in the movie might have entirely unrelated movies that you downloaded from YouTube. By identifying similar features, the computer projects its interpretation of an individual's appearance from various perspectives and environments onto the other person in the target video.

In addition, generative adversarial networks (GANs) are incorporated into the mix. GANs find and enhance any imperfections in the deepfake over several rounds, making it more difficult for deepfake detectors to decode them.

Although the software is somewhat accessible, the method is difficult. GitHub, an open source development community, has a vast collection of deepfake software. Some of these apps, including the Chinese app Zao, DeepFace Lab, FakeApp, and Face Swap, make creating deepfakes simple even for novices.[11]

Identity verification company iProov discovered in its 2024 threat intelligence report titled "The Impact of Generative AI on Remote Identity Verification" that a growing number of threat actors with a focus on deepfakes are accelerating their efforts with the help of free and inexpensive face swap tools, virtual cameras, and mobile emulators.

According to a public statement from iProov chief scientific officer Andrew Newell, "Generative AI has provided a huge boost to threat actors' productivity levels: these tools are relatively low cost, easily accessible, and can be used to create highly convincing synthesized media such as face swaps or other forms of deepfakes that can easily fool the human eye as well as less advanced biometric solutions."[12]

An example of deepfake fraud occurred recently in Hong Kong. A clerk employed by a multinational corporation in Hong Kong donated

HK$200 million of the company's funds to con artists after being duped into attending a video conference in which every other participant was an AI-generated deepfake.

The other participants in the video chat were scammer creations, posing as the worker's coworkers; the clerk was the only real person there. The other participants were fictitious accounts based on actual online conferences that had previously occurred.

> "The informant [clerk] received an invitation from [the fraudster] to a video conference with numerous participants. The informant made 15 transactions to five local bank accounts as directed, totaling HK$200 million, because the individuals in the video conference appeared to be the actual persons. I believe the fraudster downloaded videos in advance and then used artificial intelligence to add fake voices to use in the video conference," acting senior superintendent Baron Chan said.[13]

AI also affected the music world when in April 2023 Drake & The Weeknd's single "Heart on My Sleeve" was released. The collaboration of two of the industry's biggest talents didn't raise any waves. The fact that the two pop icons weren't working together rocked it.

But the reality was a person going by the moniker Ghostwriter wrote the song "Heart on My Sleeve," which amassed millions of plays on TikTok, YouTube, and Spotify before Universal Music Group pushed the sites to remove it. Ghostwriter closely mimicked Drake and The Weeknd's voices using cutting-edge AI technologies. The song was a hit even though its composition raised ethical concerns. "Heart on My Sleeve" is only a preview of what deepfakes and sophisticated generative AI are going to bring us in the future.

According to the US Department of Treasury, criminals can now more convincingly mimic speech or video to pose as clients of financial institutions and get access to accounts because of recent advances in AI. Furthermore, according to the Treasury, they enable malevolent actors to create progressively complex email phishing attacks with improved formatting and fewer errors.[14]

Another area of concern about deepfakes with generative AI is voice simulation. It can easily be used for nefarious purposes by pretending to be someone in a position of authority or importance.

A text-to-speech AI model called Voice Engine has been developed by OpenAI, and it can produce artificial voices from a 15-second audio clip. After a voice is cloned, words can be entered into the Voice Engine to produce an AI-generated voice output. OpenAI isn't yet prepared to make its technologies due to security and ethical considerations.

With just 15 seconds of a person's recorded voice, anyone may essentially clone that voice, which has clear ramifications for potential abuse. The capacity to clone voices has already produced problems in society, even if OpenAI never publishes its Voice Engine broadly. Examples include phone fraud when someone impersonates a loved one and robocalls during election campaigns that feature cloned voices from politicians.

Sen. Sherrod Brown (D-Ohio), the chairman of the US Senate Committee on Banking, Housing, and Urban Affairs, also sent a letter to the CEOs of several major banks in May 2023 asking them about the security precautions they were taking against AI-powered risks because researchers and reporters have demonstrated that voice-cloning technology can be used to break into bank accounts that use voice authentication (such as Chase's Voice ID).[15]

The legal environment surrounding deepfakes is complicated. Copyright, the right of publicity, section 43(a) of the Lanham Act, and the torts of defamation, false light, and intentional infliction of emotional distress are among the frameworks that may be invoked to counter deepfakes. The First Amendment's safeguards, copyright law's fair use theory, section 230 of the Communications Decency Act (CDA), and other laws that apply to social networking services and other websites that host content from third parties constitute the other side of the ledger.

The courts will have a difficult time striking the correct balance. Decisions that give persons targeted by deepfakes unduly broad protection run the risk of violating the First Amendment and being overturned on appeal. If deepfake targets are not sufficiently protected by rulings, people may be left without a way to counteract potentially extremely dangerous deepfakes. Additionally, attempts to reduce CDA section 230 in an effort to combat the threat posed by deepfakes would have a wide range of unanticipated and detrimental effects on the internet environment that can create false and fraudulent scenarios.[16]

In summary, concerns regarding the possibility of identity theft and other forms of fraud, as well as the spread of deepfakes and sophisticated AI-generated material, are being raised in relation to the potential for misinformation and manipulation in politics and the media. AI has the potential to increase the effectiveness of ransomware and phishing assaults by making them more resilient, persuasive, and difficult to identify.

AI Is Also Being Used by Hackers to Break Passwords More Quickly

The impact AI assaults might have on online identity security is the most immediate concern. AI's deep learning can be used guess passwords and to accelerate brute force attacks. A strong password is no longer sufficient to secure an online account; instead, modern identification systems must act swiftly to thwart automated, optimized attacks that depend on the application of industry standards that have been in place for decades.

For online identity security, multifactor authentication (MFA) has long been the preferred method. This technique is predicated on the idea that an individual must present numerous pieces of proof—such as various devices or firsthand knowledge—to establish their identity. Unfortunately, AI has the ability to create device spoofs that render this MFA useless. Additionally, as previously indicated, AI phishing messages are increasingly convincing, which facilitates the collection of personal data for security question responses.

An assessment on AI-enabled cyber threats was published by the National Cyber Security Centre (NCSC), a reputable source on the UK's cyber danger. The NCSC integrated data from all sources, including open source, academic research, industry expertise, and classified intelligence, to produce independent key judgments that guide policy decisions and enhance cybersecurity in the United Kingdom. Here are their conclusions:

- AI will almost certainly increase the volume and heighten the impact of cyberattacks over the next two years.
- The threat to 2025 comes from evolution and enhancement of existing tactics, techniques, and procedures.

- All types of cyber threat actors—state and non-state, skilled and less skilled—are already using AI, to varying degrees.
- AI provides capability uplift in reconnaissance and social engineering, certainly making both more effective, efficient, and harder to detect.
- More sophisticated uses of AI in cyber operations are highly likely to be restricted to threat actors with access to quality training data, significant expertise (in both AI and cyber), and resources. More advanced uses are unlikely to be realized before 2025.
- AI will certainly make cyberattacks against the UK more impactful because threat actors will be able to analyze exfiltrated data faster and more effectively and use it to train AI models.
- AI lowers the barrier for novice cybercriminals, hackers-for-hire, and hacktivists to carry out effective access and information-gathering operations. This enhanced access will contribute to the global ransomware threat over the next two years.
- Moving toward 2025 and beyond, commoditization of AI-enabled capability in criminal and commercial markets will certainly make improved capability available to cybercrime and state actors.[17]

In summary, generative AI technology gives hackers the ability to launch assaults more frequently with automation and with greater variety. It simply takes them thousands of socially engineered variations to produce thousands of attacks, and a target has to only fall for one phish. There are a multitude of approaches and applications of how AI attacks can break the veneer of cyber defenses.

The problem with the threats associated with generative AI is that only 17% of businesses have trained or informed their entire company on the dangers connected with generative AI, despite the fact that a staggering 93% of organizations foresee substantial hazards from this technology, according to a Riskconnect poll of 300 risk and compliance professionals. Even more concerning: just 9% of respondents believe they are equipped to handle the hazards associated with using generative AI.[18]

As the statistics have demonstrated, there has already been a clear wake-up call for companies, organizations, and governments to fortify their networks and devices against AI-enabled threats. The potential for extensive damage and disruption is a significant risk posed by attacks created by AI. Organizations need to invest in defensive AI technology, promote a security-aware culture, and update their defense plans often to be ready for these attacks. Businesses might strengthen their defenses against this novel and morphing threat by continuing to be proactive and watchful.

The next chapter will explore some ways and solutions to better guard for the AI digital future that is rapidly evolving.

CHAPTER 14

Responding to Artificial Intelligence Cyber Threats

In the never-ending struggle for tactical and technological supremacy in cybersecurity, attackers and defenders now face competition from artificial intelligence (AI) and machine learning (ML).

Being able to stay ahead of clever attackers who want to use AI (and quantum technologies) for illicit or dangerous purposes will be one of the hardest cybersecurity challenges. It is already urgently necessary to address such vulnerabilities as threat actors attack, particularly concerning vital infrastructure. Accelerated AI research and development is necessary to improve advanced capabilities and close cyber gaps, which can include weak threat intelligence and lack of modern cybersecurity technologies and training. These gaps are readily exploitable, especially in light of asymmetrical technological threats where hackers can automate attacks simultaneously to many thousands of targets, needing just one to be successful. Bolstering cybersecurity should be pursued as a priority collectively by the public and private sectors, as well as allied nations.

With a few additional precautions, preventing AI assaults is similar to preventing other types of cyberattacks. Primarily, maintaining appropriate digital security hygiene is always a smart idea. Keep your devices' antivirus software up-to-date, avoid clicking on links from unreliable sources, log out of all accounts, delete cookies after you are done using a public network or computer, and don't share your passwords with anybody. To identify and remove dangerous software, businesses should also do maintenance sweeps on their systems on a regular basis. If one is discovered, it is best to isolate that device until the issue is fixed.

Cybersecurity systems need to be regularly evaluated and updated in order to stop these machine-driven hacker attacks. It can be quite advantageous to engage with a managed service partner if an IT department lacks the necessary expertise or resources to test and update security solutions.

AI and ML turn into indispensable instruments or creative chess pieces in a cybersecurity strategy game when it comes to adjusting to novel, complex digital surroundings. To survive and prosper, it depends on the precision, speed, and caliber of the algorithms and auxiliary technologies. In a complex game, we must be alert, creative, and one step ahead to compete.

For example, email threats alone can be devastating to businesses if they lead to breaches. Businesses must enhance their security measures, and no one solution can eliminate the risks associated with AI-generated email assaults.

Cyber defenses are increasingly dependent on email filtering solutions that can employ AI to block harmful communications before they reach consumers. A holistic approach to layering emerging solutions to meet the growing AI-generated cyber threats is becoming a must for most companies.

The cybersecurity firm CrowdStrike prepared a short list of some of the benefits of using ML in cybersecurity: There are many benefits to applying ML to problems in the cybersecurity space:[1]

- **Rapidly synthesize large volumes of data.** One of the biggest challenges faced by analysts is the need to rapidly synthesize intelligence generated across their attack surface, which is typically generated much faster than their teams can manually process. ML is able to quickly analyze large volumes of historical and dynamic intelligence, enabling teams to operationalize data from various sources in near real time.
- **Activate expert intelligence at scale.** Regular training cycles enable models to continuously learn from their evolving sample population, which includes analyst-labeled detections or analyst-reviewed alerts. This prevents recurring false

positives and enables models to learn and enforce expert-generated ground truth.

♦ **Automate repetitive, manual tasks.** Applying ML to specific tasks can help alleviate security teams from mundane, repetitive tasks, acting as a force multiplier that enables them to scale their response to incoming alerts and redirect time and resources toward complex, strategic projects.

♦ **Augment analyst efficiency.** ML can augment analyst insight with real-time, up-to-date intelligence, enabling analysts across threat hunting and security operations to effectively prioritize resources to address their organization's critical vulnerabilities and investigate time-sensitive ML-alerted detections.

Security professionals need to adapt their third-party risk management strategy in light of companies' reliance on vendors for generative AI solutions. This requires addressing the inherent difficulties and presenting specific issues related to supply chain security and risk management.

A bold whitepaper from Google called "Secure, Empower, Advance: How AI Can Reverse the Defender's Dilemma" offers three substantive ways to assimilate AI into cybersecurity. The following adapted list describes these recommendations:[2]

♦ **Secure AI from the ground up.** AI-powered security must sit on a trustworthy foundation for the technology to correct some of the original shortcomings of our digital domain. Applying the lessons learned from decades of cybersecurity is vital during the excitement of this moment. Recent policy and industry efforts have focused on mitigating foundation model risks, but models are only one part of the systems that users and enterprises will interact with. Secure-by-design principles need to infuse the life cycle of the technology at all layers of the stack. And to ensure the technology can be trusted to deploy at scale, we must collaborate on developing new guardrails for autonomous cybersecurity.

♦ **Empower defenders over attackers.** Our societies need a balanced regulatory approach to AI use and adoption to avoid a future where attackers can innovate but defenders cannot.

AI governance choices made today can shift the terrain in cyberspace in unintended ways. There are a number of actions we can take today to ensure we maximize the technology's utility for defenders while minimizing malicious use. Although AI risk management is critical, certain policy approaches—such as those that limit AI use in critical infrastructure or allow users to opt out of AI security functions—will bind the hands of cyber defenders but leave attacker use of the technology unconstrained. We can work together to give defenders the upper hand—such as by pooling security-relevant data set to ensure defenders have access to better models than attackers.

♦ **Advance research cooperation to generate scientific breakthroughs.** The research community must play a significant role in enabling new paradigms for security and software development. This includes testing and evaluating new security technologies, assessing, and prioritizing risks, and introducing new innovations to help eliminate entire classes of threats.

Although existing publications tend to focus on demonstrating attacks on or using AI, we should prioritize research into building defenses against or with AI. Capturing the opportunity to shape the direction of AI-powered security will take bold investments and cooperation across governments, industries, and civil society. Reversing the defender's dilemma is an ambitious goal, and achieving it is by no means assured. Attackers will work just as hard to undermine these efforts. But this is why bold and timely action is needed today.

The managing director and main analyst of theCUBE Research, Shelly Kramer, and analyst, engineer, and member of theCUBE Collective community, Jo Peterson, have recommended the following seven cybersecurity products/vendors safeguarding generative AI:[3]

♦ **Security AI Workbench on Google Cloud.** Constructed on Duet AI within Google Cloud, the Security AI Workbench provides AI-driven functionalities to evaluate, enumerate, and rank threat information from both public and proprietary sources. Using threat intelligence from Google, Mandiant, and

Virus Total, Security AI Workbench is constructed on the Vertex AI framework. It is driven by Sec-PaLM 2, a specialized security LLM that integrates threat intelligence into the system. Additionally, it has extensions that let customers and partners build on the platform while maintaining control over and isolation of their data. Security AI Workbench offers compliance support together with enterprise-grade security, as we would expect.

- **Copilot for Security from Microsoft.** Microsoft claims that its Copilot for Security will enable users to "protect at the speed and scale of AI." Microsoft Sentinel, Defender, and Intune are all compatible with Copilot for Security, which is connected with Microsoft's security ecosystem. Copilot uses AI to automate incident response, improve threat intelligence, proactively detect cyber threats, and condense massive data signals into meaningful insights. Additionally, the solution is made so that less experienced employees can also use it with ease. It offers simple instructions that make learning and use of the solution quick and straightforward, eliminating the need for senior staff members to step in.

- **Charlotte AI from CrowdStrike.** Conversational AI is used by CrowdStrike's Charlotte AI to support security teams in moving swiftly. Customers can ask, answer, and act with Charlotte AI's NLP capabilities, which are based on the Falcon platform. According to CrowdStrike, users can minimize analyst effort and increase productivity while completing security activities up to 75% faster and assimilating thousands of pages of threat intelligence in just a few seconds. Furthermore, according to CrowdStrike, Charlotte AI can compose technical queries 57% faster—even for people with no prior experience with cybersecurity.

- **Howso.** Howso, formerly known as Diveplane, is committed to making reliable AI the norm worldwide. The Howso team is focused on providing AI that is reliable, transparent, and auditable. All they produce is based on the open source Howso Engine, an ML engine that precisely traces influence back to input data, enabling complete traceability and accountability.

The digitally created data used in the Howso Synthesizer is based on the Howso Engine, performs as expected, and poses no privacy or regulatory problems. Numerous use cases exist in the health care, government, fintech, and other domains wherein enterprises must safely analyze and exchange data with one another as well as with other entities.

- **Security Cloud by Cisco.** Designed with zero trust in mind, Cisco Security Cloud is an open, comprehensive security platform for multicloud settings. Through the integration of generative AI, the Cisco Security Cloud is enhanced in terms of threat identification, policy administration ease, and security operations simplification through the use of cutting-edge AI analytics. Cisco Security Cloud comprises the Cisco User Protection Suite, Cisco Cloud Protection Suite, and Cisco Breach Protection Suite.

- **SecurityScorecard.** Supply chain cyber risk, external security and risk operations solutions, and forward-looking threat information through the Threat Landscape product line are all included in the SecurityScorecard solutions. The organization conveniently offers insurance policies for cybersecurity as well. Chat GPT4 is used by SecurityScorecard's AI-driven platform to provide comprehensive security scores that specifically comprehend an organization's overall security posture. Customers can obtain instantaneous actionable insights by using natural language processing (NLP) queries in the tool.

- **Synthesis AI.** A proprietary blend of generative AI and cinematic DGI pipelines powers Synthesis AI's Synthesis Humans and Synthesis Scenarios, which are an extension of the company's data creation platform. For ML models, the Synthesis platform can programmatically generate precisely tagged photos; we anticipate seeing more of them in the future. For realistic security simulation and cybersecurity training, teams can also employ Synthesis Humans.

Those are good recommendations, and there are many other new products and services on the market looking to help provide cybersecurity solutions to mitigate the adversarial uses of generative AI.

Another for consideration is AI from MixMode. It was created to recognize and counteract sophisticated adversarial attacks, such as adversarial generative AI. This gives MixMode the ability to identify and eliminate risks from hostile actors and deceptive AI agents that try to enter systems and avoid detection by cleverly adapting. Security personnel are able to lock down threats before they cause damage because any unusual behavior instantly sets off notifications.

The Defense Advanced Research Projects Agency (DARPA) has transitioned newly developed defensive capabilities from a program focused on building defenses against adversarial attacks on AI systems. Officials had recognized that US military computer vision and ML technologies could be tricked so they imitated a project to help mitigate those possibilities.

Matt Turek, deputy director for DARPA's Information Innovation Office, said that

> AI systems are made out of software, obviously, right, so they inherit all the cyber vulnerabilities—and those are an important class of vulnerabilities—but [that's] not what I'm talking about here. There are sort of unique classes of vulnerabilities for AI or autonomous systems, where you can do things like insert noise patterns into sensor data that might cause an AI system to misclassify. So you can essentially by adding noise to an image or a sensor, perhaps break a downstream machine learning algorithm. You can also with knowledge of that algorithm sometimes create physically realizable attacks. So, you can generate very purposefully a particular sticker that you could put on a physical object that when the data is collected, when that object shows up in an image, that particular . . . adversarial patch makes it so that the machine learning algorithm might not recognize that object exists or might misclassify that tank as a school bus.

He also noted that "deception attacks can enable adversaries to take control of autonomous systems, alter conclusions of ML-based decision support applications, and compromise tools and systems that rely on ML and AI technologies. Current techniques for defending

ML and AI have proven brittle due to a focus on individual attack methods and weak methods for testing and evaluation."[4]

Generative AI for Cyber Defense

Security teams are becoming more precise, effective, and productive in their cyber defense efforts thanks to generative AI. Because AI and ML free up security professionals to concentrate on the most critical duties, they can help respond to threats more effectively. Security teams can concentrate on other areas that need more attention by using algorithms to automate boring or repetitive processes, including identifying harmful URLs or scanning for malware.

The following are some instances of generative AI in cyber defense.

REAL-TIME THREAT DETECTION

One of the most popular applications of generative AI nowadays is threat detection. Organizations can greatly accelerate their ability to discover new threat vectors by employing it to sift event alerts more effectively, eliminate false positives, and spot trends and anomalies faster. ML is being used more and more to find threats and eliminate them before they have a chance to cause havoc because of its capacity to sift through millions of files and identify those that may be dangerous.

Microsoft software demonstrated this ability in 2018 when hackers tried to infect over 400,000 users with a cryptocurrency miner in a 12-hour period. Microsoft's Windows Defender, a program that uses several levels of ML to recognize and block threats, prevented the attempt. The moment the cryptocurrency miners began their excavation, they were shut down.

It is anticipated that as hybrid and cloud systems gain popularity, there will be 29 billion linked devices by 2027. There is ongoing strain on ML to account for and defend additional connections against cyberattacks as a result of company networks adding new PCs, tablets, and other devices.[5]

IMPROVING THE AWARENESS OF POTENTIAL THREATS

Threat intelligence is also improved by generative AI. In the past, analysts had to examine enormous volumes of data to comprehend threats using complicated query languages, procedures, and reverse engineering. They can now make use of generative AI algorithms, which automatically look for dangers in code and network traffic and offer insightful information to assist analysts in comprehending how malicious scripts and other threats behave.

The use of AI and ML by defenders to improve security orchestration, automation, and response platforms is growing. This can be achieved by giving improved analytics to support decision-making or by just cutting down on the time and effort consumed on manual investigations.

PATCHING SECURITY FLAWS AUTOMATICALLY

Patch analysis and application processes can be automated with generative AI. It can apply or recommend suitable patches using NLP pattern matching or a ML approach where neural networks are used to scan code bases for vulnerabilities. Because of the volumes of misconfigurations and vulnerabilities discovered every day, ML can more rapidly synthesize gaps needing to be patched.

ENHANCING THE REACTION AND RESPONSES TO INCIDENTS

Incident response is a successful area in which generative AI is used in cybersecurity. Security analysts can expedite incident response times by using generative AI to create response strategies based on effective techniques from previous occurrences. Additionally, as events unfold, generative AI can keep learning from them and modify these reaction plans accordingly. Generative AI can be used by organizations to automate the generation of incident response reports.

ML combined with generative AI are becoming increasingly important in cybersecurity due to these trends in the field:

- ◆ The number of cloud- and Internet of Things–based connections is increasing as a result of employees performing tasks online more frequently due to remote work and hybrid work models.
- ◆ ML's capacity to swiftly scan and evaluate vast volumes of data is essential because systems are now producing mountains of data.

AI Security at the Hardware Level

Threat actors are becoming increasingly skilled at finding weaknesses to take advantage of AI and ML technologies. These actors include state-sponsored and criminal organizations who focus on software as well as holes in hardware. Hackers are increasingly likely to search for vulnerable ports and systems on businesses' networks, particularly industrial systems that are connected to the internet. Therefore, AI-enabled cybersecurity needs to be considered in devices at the hardware level to better mitigate attacks.

PC-based security at both the hardware and software levels is important nowadays for anyone using a home office. Intel has helped address that issue. Using the Intel vPro® platform and advanced processors, Intel has produced PCs with integrated AI cybersecurity features. AI-powered improvements to PC hardware and software can help businesses detect, prevent, and recover from intrusions. The improved multilayered threat detection methods, which include app and data protections and hardware-based safeguards that support below-the-OS security to maintain device and data integrity, make up the security integration of the Intel® vPro platform.

In the grand scheme of things, cybersecurity is all about sealing gaps and strengthening weak points that could be used by malevolent hackers. That need is urgent. AI-enabled malware has undoubtedly chosen to infiltrate systems via software. But in the current environment of cyber threats, hardware concerns cannot afford to be disregarded.

Because there are so many levels of vulnerabilities and layers for cybersecurity, I created Figure 14.1 to encapsulate in one view some of the key elements of AI and cybersecurity and how they are closely linked.

Sometimes statistics tell a story. It is evident that AI is already affecting cybersecurity, as shown in the following list:

AI in Cybersecurity: Top 10 Statistics[6]

◆ By 2030, the global AI in cybersecurity market is expected to be worth $133.8 billion.

◆ Breaches that affected organizations with fully deployed security AI solutions cost them, on average, $1.8 million less than businesses without them.

ARTIFICIAL INTELLIGENCE AND CYBERSECURITY

AI can provide a faster and automated means to detect and identify cyber threats.

Uses of Artificial Intelligence and Cybersecurity
- Threat detection (spam and phishing)
- Malware identification
- End point detection
- Spam filtering and bot identification
- Password protection and user authentication
- Autonomous patching
- Categorize attacks; lessen false/positives
- Adapt to evolving risks—predictive analytics
- Incident response

AI threat-hunting tools can cover cloud, data center, enterprise networks, and IoT devices.

AI can support cyber threat analysts and address the problem of information overload and current data.

Technology is at an inflection point in history and AI will be disrupting the digital ecosystem.

AI can be a double-edged sword as it can be manipulated for nefarious purposes.
- AI-generated malware can evade current-generation threat detection systems.
- Nation state or criminal enterprise actors can use malicious AI to hide malware in regular downloadable applications.
- Hackers can use AI as a tool to misdirect a program or application into thinking that threat activities are normal when they are not.

- AI can monitor activities in real time on networks by scanning data to recognize unauthorized communications.
- AI can help identify false positives, which is a major challenge for human analysts.
- AI can be used to strengthen access control measures.

AI advances network surveillance and threat detection tools to support cybersecurity professionals by reducing noise, providing priority alerts, and employing contextual data supported by evidence.

Infographic by Chuck Brooks
linkedin.com/in/chuckbrooks

Figure 14.1 Links between AI and cybersecurity.

♦ Organizations with AI cybersecurity took 100 days less to identify and contain these data breaches when they occurred, compared to those lacking them (IBM, 2023).

♦ Seventy-five percent of security professionals have seen an increase in cyberattacks in the past year, and 85% blame AI.

♦ Almost half (46%) of those same respondents believe generative AI will leave organizations more vulnerable to cyberattacks than they were before AI (Deep Instinct, 2023).

♦ Businesses are adopting an increasingly proactive, rather than reactive, approach to cybersecurity, with 2023 seeing a 95% increase toward this mentality vis à vis 2022 (Deep Instinct, 2023).

♦ Among cybersecurity experts' top concerns about AI implementation were increases in privacy (39%), undetectable phishing attacks (37%), and both the volume and velocity of attacks (33%) (Deep Instinct, 2023).

♦ Thirty-four percent of organizations are already using or implementing AI cybersecurity tools.

♦ Sixty-nine percent of enterprises believe AI in cybersecurity is necessary due to the burgeoning number of threats that human analysts are unable to get to.

♦ With AI, there will be a 150% increase in predictive analysis for cyber threats by 2025 (Zipdo, 2023).

Because it provides a proactive security mechanism with accurate and quick detection, cyber AI has grown in popularity. The projected growth of the AI cybersecurity market reflects those realities.

AI tools are becoming more and more popular for spotting, identifying, and mitigating online risks. The necessity for sophisticated AI in cybersecurity has been highlighted by the exponential increase in cyberattacks against government, defense, and high-tech organizations. AI applications that are targeted and focused can help combat the growing number of threats. In order to compete in this difficult environment, government organizations and business executives must move quickly and wisely to implement AI-powered solutions and approaches to boost the efficacy and efficiency of their security teams.

CHAPTER 15

Artificial Intelligence and Privacy

A rtificial intelligence (AI) privacy is a major worry. For years, a lot of businesses have shared user data with different developers and third-party businesses, putting them at risk from threat actors and data brokers.

Your online activities across many websites are being monitored almost everywhere you go. Additionally, your location is being collected if you are using a mobile app and have enabled GPS on your phone.

AI increases all of those privacy risks. Every aspect is automated and on a greater scale. There will be less choice over what personal data is gathered about you, how it's used, and whether or not it's used to train large language models. Some models could have been trained on sensitive data and end up disclosing users' personal information.

AI-generated data also presents privacy concerns, such as the need for freely provided informed consent, the ability to opt out, restrictions on data collection, explanations of the nature of AI processing, and the ability to have data deleted on request.

Because AI is constantly monitoring everything we say and do online, total privacy concerns may be an ephemeral notion in the digital age. Vint Cerf, chief evangelist at Google and one of the inventors of the internet, has already declared that privacy is extinct. He says that absence from the internet is the only method to prevent data breaches.[1]

Privacy is certainly a big concern with the use of AI, including in cybersecurity and for general operations where any personally identifiable data is involved. According to privacy expert Daniel Solove,

> AI has ushered in an unprecedented amount of data collection. Personal data for AI is gathered primarily in two ways—through scraping the data from the internet or by repurposing customer or user data. AI's thirst for data is placing tremendous stress on privacy laws, which attempt to place meaningful controls on data gathering. In many instances. AI could evade the protection of many privacy laws. In other circumstances, some laws, if strictly interpreted and enforced, would restrict the collection of data for AI, starving it of the data needed to function. Finding a middle ground between a data feeding frenzy or data famine will be difficult.[2]

But privacy is not a zero-sum game. Organizations will need to focus on data reduction to meet privacy issue expectations and comply with regulations protecting consumers. With the General Data Protection Regulation (GDPR), Europe has done a good job of at least reminding users that what they click on might be shared. In the end, the decision of what data to make available rests with the person or organization that owns the resource. To better safeguard privacy, consider data segmentation, encryption, and zero trust.

The zero trust concept was first pushed in 2010 by Forrester security analyst John Kindervag. The idea suggests protecting enterprises by shifting the focus of security from implicit trust established by the presence of gadgets within the enterprise. Rather, by taking into account the internet services linked to business networks, it goes beyond the typical boundary of what is audited in a network. It mandates that all digital transactions be viewed as untrusted when requesting services, and it gives every device, regardless of location, a no trust status. Its fundamental tenet is that security—especially cybersecurity—should not be taken lightly.

The zero trust paradigm gives cybersecurity teams more strength and empowers them to swiftly and authoritatively safeguard data security and privacy. However, it makes IT security, operations, and management's implementation load heavier. Applying zero trust without conducting adequate research and executing the plan with care might slow down business transactions, which can have a detrimental impact on margin flows.

Under zero trust for privacy, only necessary information should be collected and retained. While enabling insightful analysis, individual identities should be protected through the use of robust encryption, anonymization, and pseudonymization procedures. Furthermore, sensitive data should be available only to those who are permitted thanks to access controls and frequent authorization checks.

To find and fix privacy holes in their operations, many companies and governmental organizations use privacy impact assessments. AI can be used to assist in detecting those gaps; however, the use of AI will also change the ecosystem for those exfiltrating any personal information—a person's full name, phone number, email address. What was once considered hidden can be easily extracted from open source data or stolen data with AI tools that risk privacy.

Health Care and Privacy

Although privacy is a concern for many industries, it is especially important for health care. The increasing networked and connected nature of medical treatment through computers and other devices has made the digital environment of health administration, clinics, hospitals, and patients more vulnerable.

Cyberattacks against the health care industry have surely increased as a result of COVID-19 and the related growth in employees working remotely. An open and fragmented ecosystem as a result of more connections, endpoints, and less targeted security was exploited by hackers. In 2024, as AI grows and becomes more widely applied in the health care sector, more sophisticated hacks will occur.

Privacy protection for patients is a top concern for all parties involved in health care. Legislators and federal agencies periodically assess HIPAA compliance as well as other regulation security procedures. The HIPAA Security Rule directs the privacy and security protocols for electronic health records (EHRs). The security rule establishes federal guidelines for using technical and physical security measures to preserve the availability, confidentiality, and integrity of electronically protected health information. Hackers target EHRs as their main objective. Health records are of special value to hackers as they have a sales value on the deep web; plus, they can open the door for other avenues of exploitation such as Medicare fraud.

Attacks aren't necessarily more frequent than they have been in recent years. However, according to John Riggi, national advisor for cybersecurity for the American Hospital Association, the attacks have caused greater harm and impacted a larger number of people. In 2023, about 100 million people were affected by health care hacks.[3]

Patient privacy protection is of utmost importance to stakeholders in the health care industry. Legislators and federal agencies often evaluate other security regulations and HIPAA compliance. EHR privacy and security policies are governed by the HIPAA Security Rule. In order to maintain the accessibility, privacy, and integrity of electronically protected health information, the security rule sets forth federal principles for putting in place technical and physical security measures.

As of 2024, the US federal government lacks a comprehensive data privacy law. Congress has passed several laws establishing data obligations for specific businesses and data subcategories, but these legal safeguards are not all-inclusive. The lack of a comprehensive federal data privacy law has led some individuals and groups to address possible privacy violations of using generative AI and other AI technologies by adapting principals other legal frameworks such as copyright, defamation, and right of publicity.

But in some states, the legal environment concerning AI and data privacy is influenced by regulations such as the California Consumer Privacy Act (CCPA) in the United States and the GDPR in the European Union.

People now have more control over their data according to the GDPR, which has established a global standard for data protection. It establishes stringent criteria on the management of sensitive information, including medical records; demands express consent for data gathering; and provides rights including data erasure. In a similar vein, the CCPA grants Californians the right to refuse the sale of their personal data and to know what personal information is gathered about them.[4]

In today's society we often do not pay enough attention to the privacy of our data. Because of the implications of AI being used to gather and synthesize what we do in our personal and economic lives, privacy needs to be continually addressed in legal and legislative initiatives.

CHAPTER 16

Artificial Intelligence and Ethics

With the help of artificial intelligence (AI), we can do incredible new things to improve people's lives and the globe. To achieve it, though, would need our conscious decision to act morally.

Legal standards offer a foundation for safeguarding privacy in AI applications, but ethical issues frequently transcend legal bounds. Fairness, autonomy, privacy, and other basic human rights are among the values that ethical AI aims to balance with the advancement of technology.

In addressing those issues, we need to consider the potential ethical concerns with AI in the future when it becomes thoroughly advanced. Society is at a critical juncture in AI and must proceed cautiously and prudently. The potential consequences of implementing this technology as well as who will be in charge of it must be considered.

Governments, businesses, civil society organizations, and individuals are among the stakeholders who have to guarantee the development and application of ethical AI. Maintaining moral standards and cultural norms while using AI-driven security solutions must be done in a careful and balanced manner. Transparency, accountability, and fairness concerns need to be carefully considered as AI systems grow more independent and capable of making important judgments. Strong governance practices must be put in place by organizations to guarantee that AI-driven security measures don't unintentionally violate people's privacy, reinforce prejudices, or have other negative effects.

Designing systems that are strong and resistant to abuse will be a special duty placed on AI developers. To ensure that AI development is guided by human values and interests, strong ethical frameworks and governance procedures will need to be established. Building trust and maximizing the positive effects of AI technology on society will require tackling ethical issues, which range from protecting data privacy, and transparency, and reducing algorithmic prejudice.

AI isn't truly intelligent; it's often just as biased as the data we choose to use in our machine learning (ML) models. Because AI sometimes reflects the prejudices of those who train its computational models, public confidence in the technology has been damaged. Algorithm bias is a fundamental problem and has been repeatedly demonstrated. In an attempt to find a variety of viewpoints, MIT has examined several computer programming projects. They discovered that harmful biases were present in a lot of the programs. Technology is made by humans, and people are biased. This is the drawback of modern technology.

Large language models (LLMs) need to be addressed. The goal of ethical considerations is to keep LLMs from participating in improper or unethical acts. Developers have been able to incorporate rules and limitations that guarantee AI systems reject requests for hazardous or immoral information by honing these models. We need to make sure that these guidelines and standards continue to prevent AI from interacting and engaging with dangerous, offensive, or unlawful content as interactive AI develops and gains more autonomy than generative AI models.

The infringement of intellectual property (IP), which arises when IP (including text, music, and photos) is snatched into training engines for big language models and made available to anybody using the technology, is another ethical problem.

Generative AI systems have come under fire in an open letter for allegedly violating IP rights. An open letter signed by over 200 musicians, including well-known performers like Nicki Minaj, Billie Eilish, and Camila Cabello, requested that AI developers, tech companies, and digital platform providers cease using AI technology to steal the voices and likenesses of artists.

Leading technology corporations are accused in the letter of using the musicians' work to train AI models without their consent.

The artists also claim that businesses are attempting to tamper with the royalty pools that artists receive by creating AI-generated sounds and pictures.[1]

Copyright issues arise from AI systems' ability to create content that resembles that of human creativity. A number of recent incidents have brought attention to these issues and are some of the obstacles that business executives and legal experts must overcome.

Ensuring that AI-generated material respects IP rights and lowers the possibility of IP theft should be the ethical goal of businesses. In order to ensure that AI and human creativity coexist harmoniously, a well-balanced approach that fosters innovation and protects IP is essential. But the goal of "responsible control" isn't automatically or easily achieved. Governance and guardrails are integral to the process of how it is used for good purposes.

The big takeaway for ethics and regulatory policies is that both algorithms and LLMs can be fallible. AI is a tool that can be used for good or bad. It should involve human monitoring. Oversight of machines will be necessary as AI advances. Ensuring a diverse pool of programmers for algorithms and code is crucial.

Understanding AI's contextual nature is another issue. Algorithms with programming just display XXs and OOs. Human behavior and interaction are absent from it. Though we are not there yet, we might reach a point where behavior and interaction are built into the software. Computer Vision is giving us a glimpse of that future now.

Computer Vision: Creating an Ethical Framework

Machines can analyze and comprehend visual data from the outside world thanks to computer vision, a branch of AI. This ability has been around for decades and can potentially transform industries by offering revolutionary technology for the benefit of society.

James Conner, head of corporate engagements at Ambient.ai, provides an excellent ethical AI framework for using computer vision. He believes that it is critical to strike a balance between AI's capabilities and moral principles to guarantee that it advances society.

To influence AI policies and practices, this calls for ongoing monitoring, assessment, and public involvement. For enterprise systems to be used under a common ethical framework, international cooperation is also necessary. And by concentrating on useful applications and abiding by ethical norms, AI can help provide trustworthy ethical AI.

Here are the guiding elements of Conner's AI ethical framework:[2]

- **Transparency and explainability.** AI algorithms should be transparent, with clear information on how decisions are made.
- **Bias mitigation.** It is essential to assess and address biases in training data to prevent discrimination. Remember that AI gets it very right and very wrong based on the both the accuracy and diversity of data provided.
- **Privacy protection.** With AI processing vast amounts of data, protecting individuals' privacy rights is crucial. If this is not a foundational principle within the AI product you are working with from the beginning, then it is not likely it ever will be.
- **Security.** AI models must be secure to prevent unauthorized access and data breaches. Really sounds obvious; however, many times these are treated as cost centers and not vital to the success of the deployment.
- **Human-centered design.** AI should augment human capabilities and align with human values, ensuring human oversight. As we begin this journey we should look at our first steps as how to consider human in the loop as good best practice.
- **Inclusivity.** Development and deployment should consider diverse perspectives to prevent the perpetuation of biases. Diversity or data and perspective are critical.
- **Regulatory compliance.** Adherence to regulations related to AI ethics, data protection, and privacy is necessary. Although many of the regulations that will govern AI in the near future are still under construction, it will be even more important for practitioners to understand the ethical issues and self-regulate.

Governmental Roles in Regulating AI

AI technology is developing quickly, which presents governance and regulatory issues. It is difficult work that calls for global collaboration and forethought to create laws that effectively safeguard the public interest without impeding innovation.

A resolution regarding the responsible use of AI for global AI security was recently adopted by the United Nations. The goal of the US-drafted plan, which was approved without a vote and is cosponsored by 120 nations, is to advance "safe, secure, and trustworthy artificial intelligence."

"To refrain from or cease the use of AI systems that are impossible to operate in compliance with international human rights law or that pose undue risks to the enjoyment of human rights," the Assembly called on all member states and stakeholders. The new UN resolution's subsection 6f asks member states to "strengthen investment in developing and implementing effective safeguards, including physical security, artificial intelligence systems security, and risk management across the life cycle of artificial intelligence systems," where cybersecurity threats from AI are most directly mentioned.

A greater emphasis is placed on safeguarding personal information in other recommendations, which include "mechanisms for risk monitoring and management, mechanisms for securing data, including personal data protection and privacy policies, as well as impact assessments as appropriate," which should be implemented both after AI systems have been deployed and during testing and evaluation.[3]

Using public data to train AI models raises the possibility of data security lapses that reveal personal customer information. Businesses often add their own data to the hazards involved. According to a 2024 Cisco poll, 48% of organizations have used generative AI tools to enter private company information, and 69% are concerned that these tools could violate their legal and IP rights. Millions of customers' personal information could be compromised in a single hack, making businesses exposed.[4]

For Europe, the AI Act[5] is the first set of guidelines anticipated to have an immediate effect on the application of AI. It was passed by European legislators in March 2024. New transparency requirements and a prohibition on specific AI uses are part of the regulations, which will be implemented progressively over a number of years.

The AI Act emphasizes the importance of strong cybersecurity safeguards for high-risk systems. It supports the use of advanced security measures as a defense against possible intrusions.

Specifically, the AI Act states,

> Cybersecurity plays a crucial role in ensuring that AI systems are resilient against attempts to alter their use, behavior, performance or compromise their security properties by malicious third parties exploiting the system's vulnerabilities. Cyberattacks against AI systems can leverage AI-specific assets, such as training data sets (e.g., data poisoning) or trained models (e.g., adversarial attacks), or exploit vulnerabilities in the AI system's digital assets or the underlying ICT infrastructure. In this context, suitable measures should therefore be taken by the providers of high-risk AI systems, also taking into account as appropriate the underlying ICT infrastructure.

The AI Act also will require certain high-risk systems, which need cybersecurity risk assessments before being put on the market and throughout their life cycle.

In order to achieve long-term, sustainable economic success and competitiveness, as well as to foster public trust and maximize the positive effects of AI, good data management and AI governance are essential.

THE US GOVERNMENT

In 2024, the White House delivered an executive order (EO) that focused on AI and cybersecurity.[6] To reinforce AI safety and security regulations, the EO mandates that creators of sophisticated AIs and LLMs, like ChatGPT, share vital data, including safety test outcomes, with the US government; establish guidelines and instruments to guarantee the security of these AI systems; stop AI-engineered hazardous biological materials; stop AI-enabled deception and fraud; establish a cybersecurity program to develop AI tools and patch vulnerabilities; and it will also mandate that the White House Chief of Staff and the National Security Council draft a national security memo. The EO language specifically directs the US approach on safe, cyber-secure, and trustworthy AI:

◆ It requires that developers of the most powerful AI systems share their safety test results and other critical information with the US government. In accordance with the Defense Production Act, the order will require that companies developing any foundation model that poses a serious risk to national security, national economic security, or national public health and safety must notify the federal government when training the model and must share the results of all red-team safety tests. These measures will ensure AI systems are safe, secure, and trustworthy before companies make them public.

◆ It develops standards, tools, and tests to help ensure that AI systems are safe, secure, and trustworthy. The National Institute of Standards and Technology will set the rigorous standards for extensive red-team testing to ensure safety before public release. The Department of Homeland Security will apply those standards to critical infrastructure sectors and establish the AI Safety and Security Board. The Departments of Energy and Homeland Security will also address AI systems' threats to critical infrastructure, as well as chemical, biological, radiological, nuclear, and cybersecurity risks. Together, these are the most significant actions ever taken by any government to advance the field of AI safety.

◆ It protects against the risks of using AI to engineer dangerous biological materials by developing strong new standards for biological synthesis screening. Agencies that fund life science projects will establish these standards as a condition of federal funding, creating powerful incentives to ensure appropriate screening and manage risks potentially made worse by AI.

◆ It protects Americans from AI-enabled fraud and deception by establishing standards and best practices for detecting AI-generated content and authenticating official content. The Department of Commerce will develop guidance for content authentication and watermarking to clearly label AI-generated content. Federal agencies will use these tools to make it easy for Americans to know that the communications they receive from their government are authentic—and set an example for the private sector and governments around the world.

◆ It establishes an advanced cybersecurity program to develop AI tools to find and fix vulnerabilities in critical software, building on the Biden-Harris Administration' ongoing AI Cyber

Challenge. Together, these efforts will harness AI's potentially game-changing cyber capabilities to make software and networks more secure.

♦ It orders the development of a national security memorandum that directs further actions on AI and security, to be developed by the National Security Council and White House Chief of Staff. This document will ensure that the US military and intelligence community use AI safely, ethically, and effectively in their missions, and will direct actions to counter adversaries' military use of AI.

The Department of Homeland Security recently released its inaugural AI road map noting AI's potential across the agency's enterprise for using the technology to support criminal investigations, risk mitigation after disasters, and training.

The road map states that "cyber and physical security is foundational to the safety and security of AI. DHS and the Cybersecurity and Infrastructure Security Agency in particular will continue to work to improve the nation's overall cyber resilience and to identify and manage risks."[7]

The road map also outlines a new working group inside the Science and Technology Directorate that will eventually provide an action plan aimed at addressing issues such as pilots, AI-enabled adversaries, and algorithm training. Additionally, the directorate will establish a testbed that offers impartial assessment services.

A program to increase the identification and prosecution of crimes committed using AI technology was established by the US Department of Justice (DOJ)[8] that asked for higher punishments for some crimes with AI assistance.

Two areas where DOJ will focus its AI enforcement efforts:[9]

♦ **Election security.** AI gives foreign adversaries a multitude of ways to harm voters. Bad actors can seek to use AI to "radicalize users on social media with incendiary content created with generative AI," to "misinform voters by impersonating trusted sources and spreading deepfakes," and can use "chatbots, fake images and even cloned voices" to spread falsehoods about elections and seek to deny people their right to vote.

◆ **National security.** In February 2023, DOJ and the Commerce Department announced the "Disruptive Technology Strike Force," an effort to enforce export control laws "to strike back against adversaries trying to siphon off America's most advanced technology and use it against us." This strike force "will place AI at the very top of its enforcement priority list."

The US government is also working closely with the leading AI companies on regulatory issues. Amazon, Anthropic, Google, Inflection, Meta, Microsoft, and OpenAI agreed to eight voluntary commitments concerning the use and oversight of generative AI, including watermarking. Later, eight more companies agreed to the voluntary standards: Adobe, Cohere, IBM, NVIDIA, Palantir, Salesforce, Scale AI, and Stability AI.

The eight AI safety commitments include the following:

◆ Internal and external security testing of AI systems before their release
◆ Sharing information across the industry and with governments, civil society, and academia on managing AI risks
◆ Investing in cybersecurity and insider threat safeguards, specifically to protect model weights, which affect bias and the concepts the AI model associates together
◆ Encouraging third-party discovery and reporting of vulnerabilities in their AI systems
◆ Publicly reporting all AI systems' capabilities, limitations, and areas of appropriate and inappropriate use
◆ Prioritizing research on bias and privacy
◆ Helping to use AI for beneficial purposes such as cancer research
◆ Developing robust technical mechanisms for watermarking

The full White House Fact Sheet explains in detail the voluntary commitments.[10]

The voluntary initiative by the White House and industry is a thoughtful approach to privacy, security, and regulation that must be taken to counterbalance the enormous benefits that AI offers.

Such initiatives by the government are a step in the right direction. Establishing policies and procedures that support responsible AI development and application requires cooperation with regulatory agencies, business leaders, and other stakeholders. Together, we can overcome these obstacles and mold AI's future in a way that is both morally and practically advantageous.

CHIEF DIGITAL OFFICER ROLES FOR AI

The position of chief digital officer (CDO) first appeared on corporate organizational charts about 2010 in order to adapt to the numerous changes being made in the constantly changing digital ecosystem.[11] It was a novel inclusion in government and C-suite settings. Due to the generative AI's rapid advancement, the CDO position has grown to include additional responsibilities, such as the use of data in conjunction with developing technologies, particularly AI, to gain a deeper understanding of the capabilities, dangers, and processes that make up the digital ecosystem.

Understanding the objective and having the ability to appropriately nurture and assess data and internal resources are essential for the CDO role in this new technological era. In order to construct analytics layers, the present management oversees the implementation of automation and AI skills with unattached and unstructured data sources. By leveraging AI tools, and employing their operational uses, the CDO improves the executive process's efficiency, openness, scalability, and governance, giving data and programmatic activities more meaning in the digital age.

This growing business pattern of hiring CDOs has also influenced the government. Every government department that needs the CDO's assistance has a different set of goals and data requirements. The CDO's job is to serve as a guide to make sure the digital transformation is headed in the right direction. Numerous US federal agencies have posted openings for CDOs, some of which combine director posts with AI.

Prioritizing data interchange with the many departments and offices and maintaining a valuable enterprise-wide data inventory are the responsibilities of the CDO in the public sector. The chief information security officer, chief information officer, chief technology officer, and privacy officer should work together with a CDO to ensure that standards are consistent.

Zero trust mandates in digital transformation had a significant impact on the growth of the CDO job to promote mandates. NIST defines zero trust as "The term for an evolving set of cybersecurity paradigms that move defenses from static, network-based perimeters to focus on users, assets, and resources."[12] A zero trust presupposes that no implicit confidence is given to assets or user accounts based only on the assets' ownership or physical or network location.

With zero trust and security by design becoming more and more mandated, the creation of the CDO position is evidence of the increased importance that data management and cybersecurity are gaining in the public and private sectors in order to secure data and make smart, strategic decisions.

The Department of Defense's description of the chief digital and artificial intelligence office (CDAO)[13] is a useful example for government agencies looking to get insight into the significance of CDOs and how they will develop in their functions in light of future technologies like AI:

CDAO Mission
The CDAO will accelerate DoD adoption of data, analytics, and artificial intelligence from the boardroom to the battlefield to enable decision advantage.

CDAO Vision
The CDAO envisions a modern and agile Department of Defense that fully delivers on the National Defense Strategy through a robust digital hierarchy of needs that enables Department leaders and warfighters to make proactive, timely, and impactful decisions in the boardroom and on the battlefield.

The CDAO has five primary functions:

1. Lead and oversee DoD's strategy development and policy formulation for data, analytics, and AI.
2. Work to break down barriers to data and AI adoption within appropriate DoD institutional processes.

3. Create enabling digital infrastructure and services that support Components' development and deployment of data, analytics, AI, and digital-enabled solutions.
4. Selectively scale proven digital and AI-enabled solutions for enterprise and joint use cases.
5. Surge digital services for rapid response to crises and emergent challenges.

In an effort to oversee the government's various AI efforts and reduce any potential hazards related to the rapidly developing technologies, the White House has required that chief AI officers be nominated by all federal agencies. The new OMB directive also requires federal agencies to establish AI governance committees in order to coordinate and create policies for the use of AI technologies across the board.

It seems unlikely that the CDO and CDAO roles will stop growing in significance and responsibility, even if they are still relatively new in both the government and the C-suite. These new positions and titles will become essential to handle the problems of the future as emerging technologies, particularly AI, quickly transform our society.

AI and the Prospects for the Future

AI is a driving force behind technological advancement, not just a fad. The massive expansion of people, data, connections, terminals, apps, and other elements brought about by the digitalization wave requires processing power.

Technology is reaching an inflection point in its history. AI is a driving force behind advancement in every industry sector. Traditional computing techniques have been superseded by AI and ML, which have altered daily operations across numerous sectors. AI technologies and applications have begun to transform everything operationally in a comparatively short time, from manufacturing and research to upgrading the financial and health care sectors.

As the digital era develops, we are witnessing uncontrollably rapid change catalyzed by sensors and AI. Our interactions with gadgets, the internet, and our smartphones are being affected by this change in how we communicate. Developments in technology, especially in the field of sensors, are facilitating trends in mobility and communication.

In 2022 letter, Jamie Dimon, CEO of JPMorgan Chase, referred to generative AI as "critical" to the bank's future success and compared the potentially revolutionary effects of AI to those of the "printing press, the steam engine, electricity, computing and the Internet, among others." The bank has more than doubled the number of its data scientists and AI/ML specialists in the past year, and it has expanded the applications of the technology throughout its divisions.

Dimin also stated that, "Over time, we anticipate that our use of AI has the potential to augment virtually every job, as well as impact our workforce composition. Some jobs may be created, and others may be lost as a result of it."[14]

AI's data analysis and intelligent decision-making results from the fusion of AI technology with flexible sensors. Sensors are capable of detecting multidimensional information and have three senses: smell, hearing, and sight. There are many different types and sizes of sensors, but thanks to materials science and electronics, they are becoming lighter, smaller, and more powerful. Our smartphones, clothes, and bodies can all be easily connected to them. The main use of a sensor is to measure and respond to changes in the physical environment . Motion sensors, audio sensors, and touch or magnetic sensors are a few examples. As trillions of sensors connect the world, jeopardizing security and privacy, but these tools also allow us to flourish.

An important advancement on the Internet of Things (IoT) space is the integration of edge AI with sensors. Efficiency, security, and the user experience are all improved when devices are able to make autonomous decisions in real time based on sensor data. Intelligent data processing and decision-making on edge devices are made possible by edge AI, which fundamentally blends edge computing and AI technologies.

Security of the IoT will be largely dependent on how these sensors are connected and how the data analytics are processed thereafter. Every company, organization, or government will have access to an infinite supply of crucial, timely data.

Rapid decision assistance is becoming far more useful because of new developments in data analytics that are derived from fixed and mobile sensors in the IoT combined with AI. Minutes can be spent receiving and extensively analyzing data that would typically take days to obtain. Simplified data collection, storage, preservation, management, and analysis are all going to be possible because of emerging technologies.

In fact, AI applications are developing more quickly than society can comprehend or absorb them, but at the same time, AI-powered computing systems are becoming more important and commonplace. Although these new powers have the potential to improve global safety, affordability, justice, and environmental sustainability, they also present new security risks that might endanger both public and private life.

The earnest hope lies in our ability to take this incredible technology and lead it toward ethical positive outcomes. The well-known futurist Michio Kaku describes the current technological transition as a transition from the "age of discovery" to the "age of mastery."[15] We need to use technology to our advantage and take charge of our own fate, but we must make the right choices.

A positive example of AI technology is shared by the clothing firm Levi's chief financial officer, Harmit Singh, who stated that the company's investments in digital technology, including as AI and predictive analytics, had enabled Levi's to respond swiftly to the COVID-19 outbreak when customers flocked to e-commerce platforms in large numbers.[16]

In response to market demand, the company started completing online orders using products from its stores as well as fulfillment centers. Before the health crisis, according to Singh, figuring out the logistics of a transfer like this would have taken weeks or months; however, as the epidemic spread across the nation, Levi's was able to complete the transition in a matter of days. Curbside pickup was swiftly introduced at about 80% of its 200 or so US-based stores. Even though the company released its mobile app prior to the emergence of COVID-19, it has cleverly used it to engage with customers throughout the pandemic. He states, "It was crucial for us to improve customer engagement and maintain contact with those who were at home."[17]

Such advances are happening (or will soon happen) across many industries. The White House National Science and Technology

Council Subcommittee on Machine Learning and Artificial Intelligence was established to monitor state-of-the-art advances and technology milestones. AI and ML drives improvements and new solutions to business problems across a vast array of business and social scenarios:

◆ Automation
◆ Drug research
◆ Customer relationship management
◆ Supply chain optimization
◆ Predictive maintenance
◆ Operational effectiveness
◆ Workforce effectiveness
◆ Fraud detection
◆ Automated vehicles
◆ Resource optimization

AFFECTIVE COMPUTING AND THE EXPLORATION OF LANGUAGE MODELS

Affective computing is heuristic for AI in that it studies the development of systems and devices that mimic human abilities to recognize, interpret, process, and simulate. It has evolved from an interdisciplinary field spanning computer science, psychology, and cognitive science.

For example, affective computing is revolutionizing how robots perceive and respond to human emotions. This field is poised to transform interactions in health care, customer service, and virtual reality with advances in emotion identification, ethical principles, and immersive technologies.

Creating computer systems that are either naturally emotional or that can realistically mimic emotions is a prominent field in affective computing design. Affective computing will have the ability to greatly improve human-machine interactions, which heavily depend on emotional intelligence. Political speeches, music, theater, and visual arts will use affective computing to improve emotional expression and forecast emotional responses.

With developments in affective virtual reality, emotion-assisted decision-making, empathetic human-computer communication, and affective brain-computer interfaces, the potential uses of affective computing in a variety of fields are promising. Clinical diagnoses, treatment, and military applications will all benefit from the measurement and regulation of emotional states made possible by affective brain-computer interfaces, which use neurological impulses. Empathic human-computer communication uses multimodal emotional cues to simulate human interactions and has applications in intelligent customer service and senior companionship.

By incorporating emotional factors into machine decision-making processes, emotion-aided decision-making has the potential to improve results in areas such as assisted driving and manufacturing safety. By using emotionally complex avatars to captivate users, affective virtual reality plays a critical role in creating immersive metaverses that support applications in virtual socialization, marketing, and anchors.[18]

MIMICKING NEURAL NETWORKS OF THE HUMAN BRAIN
The exploration of AI and language models demonstrates an ongoing process of learning about neural networks and the human brain. Spatial navigation has now been modeled using deep learning, an AI technique. The technology creates a spatial representation resembling the grid cells seen in mammalian brains.

In order to model neural networks at the size of the human brain, researchers at Western Sydney University in Australia have partnered with tech leaders Intel and Dell to develop a huge supercomputer. According to its claims, the DeepSouth computer can simulate networks of firing neurons at a staggering 228 trillion synaptic operations per second, which is comparable to the speed at which the human brain is thought to perform its functions.

The researchers have the goal of "progress our understanding of the brain and develop brain-scale computing applications in diverse fields including sensing, biomedical, robotics, space, and large-scale AI applications."[19]

HOW FAST WILL AI ADVANCE?
AI is on the brink of an exponential "intelligence explosion," according to the computer scientist and CEO who coined the phrase *artificial general intelligence (AGI)*. "It seems fairly possible we may get

to human-level AGI within, let's say, the next three to eight years," according to Ben Goertzel, a PhD mathematician and futurist, concluding a summit on AI.[20]

Goertzel has been researching a notion he refers to as artificial super intelligence, which he describes as an AI sufficiently sophisticated as to equal the combined mental and computational capacities of the whole human race. Goertzel stated that his argument is supported by "three lines of converging evidence."

First, he referenced the most recent research by Ray Kurzweil, Google's longtime resident futurist and computer scientist, who created a prediction model indicating that AGI will be possible by 2029. Kurzweil's theory, described in detail from his upcoming book *The Singularity Is Nearer*, was informed in part by statistics demonstrating the exponential nature of technological advancement in other tech-related industries.[21]

Others have echoed the alarming perspectives of Goertzel and Kurzweil, including Ex-Google CEO Eric Schmidt, who said AI could endanger humanity within five years, as he likens devastation to nuking Nagasaki and Hiroshima.[22]

AI is a profound subject that touches on aspects of human nature that are generally confined to philosophy, spirituality, and religion. If and when our own creations surpass us in all that we accomplish, what will become of human destinies and meaning?

INVESTMENTS IN AI ARE SOARING

It is wise to follow the money trail to see where the future of technology is going. In "Artificial Intelligence—The Next Frontier for Investment Management Firms," research by Deloitte Global,[23] the four transformational pillars are highlighted as providing organizations with the ability to create new value propositions and methods of delivering them:

> **Generating alpha:** For firms seeking organic growth through outperformance, adopting alternative data sets and AI have proved to be a differentiating factor for generating additional alpha.

> **Enhancing operational efficiency:** Firms will continue to deploy AI and advanced automation to continuously improve

the efficiency of their operations. Beyond this, firms can transform these traditional cost centers into AI-enabled "as a service" offerings.

Improving product and content distribution: Customer experience is a new battleground and AI is helping advisors to generate more insights, customize content more effectively, and deliver it to clients with greater agility and speed.

Managing risk: AI is a game changer for risk management. AI equips firms with the tools to bolster compliance and risk management functions, augment and automate data analysis, and anticipate and manage ambiguous events.

According to the report, investment management organizations might quickly improve their internal capabilities, business models, and operations by integrating AI into those four pillars. But, in order to reap the full benefits of AI, businesses will need to properly assess and manage the talent-technology nexus.

Goldman Sachs estimated that AI investment forecast will approach $200 billion globally by 2025. A report by Goldman Sachs economists Joseph Briggs and Devesh Kodnani states that "generative AI has enormous economic potential and could boost global labor productivity by more than 1 percentage point a year in the decade following widespread usage."

The economists claim that in order to purchase and integrate new technologies and restructure business processes, companies will need to make big up-front expenditures in human, digital, and physical capital. By 2025, those investments—which can total about $200 billion globally—will most likely be made before adoption and efficiency improvements begin to significantly increase productivity.[24]

Microsoft and OpenAI are developing plans for a data center project that might cost up to $100 billion and feature the 2028 debut of the "Stargate" AI supercomputer. The need for AI data centers—which can do more complex jobs than standard data centers—has skyrocketed because to the rapid adoption of generative AI technology. The project, which is anticipated to be 100 times more expensive than some of the largest current data centers, would probably be financed by Microsoft.[25]

The Saudi Arabian government intends to establish a $40 billion fund specifically for AI investments. A possible collaboration between Andreessen Horowitz, one of Silicon Valley's leading venture capital firms, and other financiers has been considered by representatives of Saudi Arabia's Public Investment Fund.

Saudi Arabia will become the global leader in AI investment thanks to the proposed tech fund. Wall Street institutions are assisting in the formation of the Saudi tech fund. Potential partners have been informed by Saudi representatives that their nation is interested in investing in a variety of AI-related start-ups, such as chip manufacturers and the pricey, large data centers that will increasingly be required to power the next generation of computing.[26]

Canada recently said that it will use $1.76 billion (or CAN$2.4 billion dollars) of its federal budget to support the AI industry and preserve its "competitive edge." To "secure Canada's AI advantage," the government presented a new set of initiatives that included investments in medium-sized companies, start-ups, and research organizations. In 2017, Canada unveiled the Pan-Canadian Artificial Intelligence plan, which intends to drive AI adoption through research and commercialization. The country claims to have been the first in the world to develop a national AI plan.[27]

AI AND THE FUSION OF OTHER TECHNOLOGIES
In the next 10 years, it should be possible to obtain computers that can perform calculations faster than a quadrillion times per second. To automate knowledge labor, we will also rely on creative software solutions for computers. Our future computing will be supported by AI technologies that enhance cognitive performance across all envisioned industry verticals.

Combining AI with classical, biological, chemical, and quantum computing will transform computer paradigms beyond recognition. AI has the potential to direct and improve quantum computing, operate on 5G or 6G networks, support the IoT, and drive the fields of materials science, biotechnology, genomics, and metaverse.

AI is going to affect many industries. For example:

◆ **Education.** To better identify students who are struggling or bored and tailor the experience to their individual requirements, AI is being used to digitize textbooks, supplement human instructors through early-stage virtual tutors, and monitor student moods using facial analysis.

◆ **Health care.** In the relatively new area of AI in health care, AI is transforming diagnosis and treatment in the medical field. Medical practitioners may now examine enormous volumes of patient data to spot patterns and anticipate possible health problems thanks to ML algorithms. Diseases can be diagnosed more quickly and correctly, medication discovery is expedited and streamlined, virtual nursing aides monitor patients, and big data analysis helps to deliver a more personalized patient experience.

◆ **Logistics and transportation.** Though they might take some time to build, autonomous cars will carry us someday. Cars will be able to negotiate traffic, minimize accidents, and maximize fuel efficiency when AI is operating them. Self-driving cars have the ability to completely transform our transportation system, which might also revolutionize the way we commute.

◆ **Manufacturing.** Predictive analytic sensors ensure that machinery is kept in excellent operating order, and AI-powered robots operate alongside humans to complete a limited range of tasks like assembling and stacking.

◆ **Customer service.** To set appointments, Google is creating an AI assistant that can speak on the phone like a human. In addition to words, the technology can understand context and subtleties.

◆ **Media.** Journalists are and will continue to use AI. Bloomberg employs Cyborg technology to aid users with rapidly comprehending intricate financial information. The natural language processing (NLP) capabilities of Automated Insights enable the Associated Press to produce nearly four times as many earning report items annually (3,700).[28]

One area to watch is robotics. Robotics and AI are merging quickly, providing a wealth of innovations that have the potential to completely transform a wide range of sectors. Their amazing effects are already being felt in several industries, including manufacturing and health care.

Key AI technologies including computer vision, ML, and NLP enable advanced robotic capabilities. These would enable robots to learn from their surroundings and make judgments and interact with people naturally. Turnkey robotics systems use AI so that robots can comprehend their surroundings and make decisions just like people.

Because humanoid robots are becoming more and more capable of capturing our interest, robotics is frequently seen as the face of emerging technology. Furthermore, they have been used for many years to automate routinely programmable tasks in manufacturing, agriculture, warehousing, health care, security, and other areas. Robotics is revolutionizing numerous industry sectors today, helped along by AI, ML, vision, and sophisticated sensors.

According to Pieter Abbeel, a professor of electrical engineering and computer science at the University of California, Berkeley, where he is also the director of the Berkeley Robot Learning Lab, "By combining machine vision with learning capabilities, roboticists are opening a wide range of new possibilities like vision-based drones, robotic harvesting, robotic sorting in recycling, and warehouse pick and place. We're finally at the inflection point: The moment where these applications are becoming good enough to provide real value in semi-structured environments where traditional robots could never succeed."[29]

A humanoid robotic version of the Terminator has also become within technological reach. Engineers at Cornell University have created a robot capable of detecting when and where it has been damaged and then restoring itself on the spot.[30]

The extent that humans are replaced by robot helpers or morphed into people-machines is an interesting philosophical question. Joan Slonczewski, a microbiologist at Kenyon College, notes that humans have continuously redefined intelligence and transferred those tasks to machines. Slonczewski asks, "Could we evolve ourselves out of existence, being gradually replaced by the machines?"[31]

Undoubtedly, science and the advancement of technology will witness fascinating and potentially transformative changes for humanity in the years to come. Our civilization has only just begun to explore the potential effects that emerging technological applications may have on our way of life, especially when applications are enhanced by AI. Fusion of technologies with AI offers much promise on optimization and development of new applications.

CHAPTER 17

The Interface Between Humans and Computers

This chapter investigates the human-computer interface, which has the potential to expand human memory and brain capacity. Modern artificial intelligence (AI) systems are powered by neural networks. AI system design and advancements are mostly inspired by the brain, which helps us comprehend the brain and its functioning. Neuromorphic computing, a technology that enables human-computer contact through AI, has the potential to enhance human brain functions, memories, and talents.

In the area of brain-computer interface, science has already made considerable progress. Brain mapping and neuromorphic chips are examples of this. Emerging assistive technology with implantable sensors that capture brain electrical signals and use them to power external devices is what gives rise to brain-computer interfaces.

Neuromorphic chips are already being produced by large tech companies. Using 64 of its Loihi neuromorphic chips, Intel created Pohoiki Beach, an 8 million synapse system with 8 million neurons (which it expects to reach 100 million neurons in the near future). Researchers are currently using Loihi chips, for example at the Telluride Neuromorphic Cognition Engineering Workshop, to construct powered prosthetic limbs and artificial skin.

TrueNorth, an IBM neuromorphic system, was introduced in 2014 and has 64 million neurons and 16 billion synapses as of this writing. IBM recently announced a collaboration with the US Air Force

Research Laboratory to construct a "neuromorphic supercomputer" known as Blue Raven, despite the company remaining relatively silent about TrueNorth's progress. The group is still investigating applications for the technology, but one possibility is to build drones that are more intelligent, lighter, and require less energy.[1]

It has even been demonstrated that a brain-computer interface is capable of reading thoughts. In order to detect electrical activity, an electrode plate known as an electrocorticography (ECOG) is placed in direct contact with the surface of the brain. According to Dr. Brian Brown, a professor at the Icahn School of Medicine at Mount Sinai, people who are paralyzed via ECOG can now converse with others by having their thoughts converted into text. In virtual environments, where people can reimagine themselves to carry out a variety of "super" activities not possible in the real world, Brown asserts that "the next step will be plugging into your brain for navigating."[2]

The promise of the human-computer interface was summarized in a *Frontiers in Science* publication that involved the cooperation of academic institutions, institutes, and scientists. "We can imagine the possibilities of what may come next with the human brain-machine interface," they said in their conclusion.[3] With instantaneous access to draw inferences from all of the human information stored in the cloud, a human B/CI system facilitated by neural nanorobotics has the potential to enhance human intellect and learning capacities. Additionally, it might raise the bar for immersive virtual and augmented reality to previously unheard-of heights, enabling users to express themselves more fully and richly and to have more meaningful experiences. These improvements might make it easier for people to use newly developed AI systems as tools for human augmentation, helping to lessen the impact of emerging threats of losing their jobs and roles in society to AI.[4]

Elon Musk recently revealed that his neuroscience start-up, NeuraLink, has developed a technology that will allow people to control computers with their minds through surgically implanted electrodes.[5] NeuraLink was founded to produce cranial computers that can upload and process information quickly. The idea of connecting computers and brains is no longer limited to science fiction.

The exciting possibilities are presented by the quickly developing field of human-machine interfaces. We are gradually approaching the ideal of the iron person, who stands as the pinnacle of human enhancement through machine and AI.

Artificial neural networks have also been used to help identify and detect human diseases by analyzing data from various medical examinations, such as CT scans, ultrasound images, and X-rays. Developments in artificial neural networks (ANN) might eventually help detect diseases before symptoms manifest or prevent diseases by identifying patients at risk of specific diseases or genetic mutations, for example.[6]

The journal *Nature Medicine* presented a case study on the application of artificial neural networks to disease prediction. This study used data from nocturnal breathing to predict and detect Parkinson's disease (PD) in patients and to track the disease's progression using artificial neural networks (ANNs). A total of 7,671 PD patients' data were used to train the ANN.[7]

Much research is being done on neuromorphic computing. As part of the Defense Advanced Research Projects Agency (DARPA) Systems of Neuromorphic Adaptive Plastic Scalable Electronics (SyNAPSE) project, researchers from the two institutions are collaborating to create a computer that can replicate human sensation, perception, action, interaction, and understanding of various stimuli. SyNAPSE aims to reverse-engineer the brain's computing capabilities. Since 2008, DARPA has invested more than $53 million in this project. (The other SyNAPSE project run by DARPA is headed by HRL Laboratories.)[8]

Neuromorphic computing will greatly accelerate our civilization's technological progress. Some futurists do not think AI is a long way off before it can qualify itself as being synonymous with human thinking and learning and even being comparable to the biology of the human brain.

It is possible that an artificial mind will possess sensory modalities beyond our comprehension, able to interpret information from a huge variety of sensors and combine it to create whole new perceptual experiences.

At a seminar on the future of the world in 2045, Ray Kurzweil, a futurist from Google, predicted that humanity will "expand the scope of our intelligence a billion-fold" and that computing power will double every two years on average.[9]

2045 is just around the corner!

Biology of Humans and Machines

Medical science has numerous applications in the field of biological and human applications. This covers wearables that can be placed within the human body, cellular implants, genome sequencing and gene editing, and precision medicine. Targeting certain bacterial strains using nano-scale medicine delivery, such as antibiotic "smart bombs," is a medical field of experimentation. Bionic eyes, bionic kidneys, and other artificially created and regenerated human organs will soon be implantable. Put simply, the human environment is about to undergo a major upgrade. It really is groundbreaking.

Over the coming years, this transformation will grow at an exponential rate. Electric, magnetic, and mechanical transductions—signatures of our biological intelligence—will be retrieved and combined with artificial circuitry. It will be similar to collecting bits of cells—including our tissue-resident stem cells—and deciphering their "code" for being in a healthy, diseased, or healing condition, or a code for being able to differentiate into all of the adult body cells. This procedure will be a first-ever method of catching a peek of the human identity.

Biocomputers might eventually be able to store data on living cells' DNA. With the use of this technology, biocomputers could be able to store practically infinite amounts of data and carry out sophisticated computations that are currently unattainable.

An inside bacterial cell serves as the basis for the biological computer that Technion researchers have previously built. They created a sophisticated biocomputer, or a biological system with programming that can perform intricate tasks. The conducted study was published in September 2019 in the journal *Nucleic Acids Research (NAR)* by PhD candidate Natalia Barger and assistant professor Ramez Daniel, who oversees the Synthetic Biology and Bioelectronics Lab at the Technion's Faculty of Biomedical Engineering "In the live cells, we constructed a kind of biological computer. Circuits do complex calculations in this computer, as they do in other computers," explained Barger. "Only here, these circuits are genetic, not electronic, and information are carried by proteins and not electrons."[10]

The current exploration of human-machine synergy gives us a peek of what lies ahead. Clearly, the prospect is thrilling from the standpoint of human augmentation. Future moral concerns will include safeguarding the rights of cyborgs, controlling super AI, and a plethora of other connected ethical matters. Human-machine interface will play a role in shaping our future. Our attention should be on how we can use it for good. Maybe that's what the Fifth Industrial Revolution will make official.

And with the emergence of all technologies comes the fusion of how they might work together. AI is no doubt one of the primary catalysts involved in enhancing capabilities, especially in computing. The advent of transformational technologies and, in particular, the increasing capacity to integrate functions as a result of exponential advancements in computing, data analytics, and material science are new tools in the systems integration toolkit. Our future fates are already being significantly shaped by these new talents.

We have benefited much from and will continue to benefit from the system's integration process. However, it needs to be enhanced. We are in the midst of a scientific revolution that frequently involves the fusion of digital and physical realms, sometimes known as techno-fusion, which is essentially a trend that tries and goes beyond conventional methods of integration, much like techno-fusion in music. I think the following five categories, out of many, serve as excellent illustrations of the shifting paradigm. These include robotics, AI, machine learning (ML), quantum and supercomputing, smart cities, and the Internet of Things; health, medicine, and life sciences technologies; and advanced imaging science. For more on this topic of fusion, please see my *Forbes* article, "The New Techno-Fusion: The Merging of Technologies Impacting Our Future.[11]

These interconnected tools for AI and computing technology could pave the way for new developments in a variety of fields, including big data, digital security, robotics, genetic engineering, augmented reality, and quantum computing.

CHAPTER 18

Artificial Intelligence and Health Care

Artificial intelligence (AI) and health can have an impact on each other in two ways. First is the threat to hospitals and health care facilities from cyberattacks, and the potential damage that can therefore occur. Second is the enormous impact AI is already making on accelerating treatment capabilities and enabling the quality of health care.

Cyber Threats

Health care executives, hospitals, and patients are all part of a digital ecosystem that is becoming increasingly vulnerable. Hospitals are vulnerable to cyberattacks due to the volume of data they handle and the numerous weak points in their various systems. Attacks with ransomware have become the go-to tactic for extortion and attacks against the health care industry.

Cybersecurity in the health care industry is changing and complex. Issues include patient privacy protection, medical equipment and device security, and information security networks of hospitals and medical facilities. The cornerstones of the transformation in health care cybersecurity are people, procedures, and technologies.

In actuality, hospitals make sense as targets for hackers due to several factors. The numerous data flows among the different systems make them vulnerable to insider threats and phishing attempts. Their networked systems with numerous stations and devices make them a prime target for ransomware and virus extortion. Furthermore, the majority of medical facility employees lack basic cybersecurity hygiene training.

Health care facilities are seen by hackers as reachable targets where they may make quick cash. Medical records that have a resale value on the dark web can be stolen by hackers. Furthermore, there is a good chance that hospital administrators might pay ransoms to regain operational control over their facilities and minimize risks to patient safety. In addition to wanting to safeguard their reputations, hospitals and other health care facilities also prefer to keep cybersecurity problems private.

AI Transforming Health Care

AI is already transforming health care through its application in medication discovery and analysis of mixtures of substances and procedures that will improve human health and combat illnesses and pandemics. AI was crucial in helping medical professionals respond to the COVID-19 pandemic and in the development of COVID-19 vaccination drugs. According to McKinsey, research and development alone can save up to $200 million globally in tuberculosis research and development costs and boost productivity gains in pharmaceutical and medical R&D by up to 20%.

Specifically, McKinsey believes that generative AI has the potential to improve a public health organization's ability to do the following:[1]

- **Engage with patients and people in various communities.** Examples include more-efficient personalized inquiry responses, enhanced chatbot performance, and improved access to quick, reliable information.
- **Synthesize concise insights.** Gathering large volumes of information and distilling insights can improve decision-making and save time, for example, by accelerating the writing and reviewing of grants. Generative AI is expected to lead to productivity gains of 15% to 20% in pharmaceutical and medical-product R&D, and a substantial portion of these gains

could come from automatically drafting clinical study reports that accelerate regulatory submissions. This could translate to savings of approximately $100 million to $200 million in worldwide tuberculosis R&D alone.

◆ **Create more tailored content.** For example, using generative AI to draft and edit text, images, and other media could lead to a 5% to 15% savings in public engagement spending through more-efficient content generation. If applied to 2021 US federal government spending on vaccine-related campaigns, this could have led to annual savings of between $85 million and $300 million, according to McKinsey analysis.

◆ **Produce efficiencies in generating and updating code.** Generative AI–based tools enable tremendous productivity gains by helping developers expedite manual and repetitive work, jump-start first drafts of code, support code completion, accelerate updates to existing code, and more readily tackle new challenges (for example, by helping developers rapidly brush up on an unfamiliar code base or language).

AI systems can analyze continuously changing data on hospital-borne infections, recovery times from medical procedures, and lengths of stay for patients to identify important patterns and subsequently make use of this information.

Predictive analytics is one of the most interesting applications of AI in health care. Using past information regarding a patient's ailments and medical interventions, predictive analytics forecasts future results depending on the patient's present state of health or symptoms. This enables medical professionals to choose the best course of action for people with recurrent medical conditions or chronic illnesses. Research in science and medicine would benefit from the computers developed by Google's DeepMind AI division, which has recently been able to predict millions of protein shapes.

AI will get more sophisticated at controlling sickness, creating individualized care plans, and forecasting health outcomes as it develops. Health care professionals will be able to treat patients more effectively at home, at charitable or religious institutions, and in the office with this ability at their disposal.

Health care, analysis, and treatment can all be made better with generative AI, but generative AI brings new cybersecurity risks to the health care industry as well. These include new ways for native generative AI attacks to work like data poisoning and prompt injection, which are ways that malicious inputs are used to change how AI responds.

CHAPTER 19

The Internet of Things

The Internet of Things (IoT) presents one of the most formidable security concerns of all. The term broadly refers to hardware and gadgets that can be found, identified, addressed, read, and/or controlled online. This encompasses tangible entities that exchange information with one another, such as the machine for humans and the machine for other machines. It encompasses everything from autos to wearable technology, from edge computers to household gadgets. IoT is the merging of the digital and real worlds.

These days, the odds are that any item that can be powered on can also be linked to the internet. The IoT enables fast and effective communication between people, objects, and objects.

What Is the Internet of Things?

Knowing what constitutes the IoT is critical for cybersecurity. IoT devices are made up of web-enabled smart devices that have embedded systems, such as CPUs, sensors, and communication hardware. These devices can be configured to work together to gather, send, and process environmental data. Through an IoT gateway, which acts as a central hub for data transfer, they establish a connection.

By 2025, there should be about 80 billion connected IoT devices, according to research firm IDC. Also, according to IDC, the number of devices connected to the internet, including the machines, sensors, and cameras that make up the IoT, continues to grow at a steady pace. IDC estimates that there will be 41.6 billion connected

IoT devices, or "things," generating 79.4 zettabytes of data in 2025. "By 2025, an average connected person anywhere in the world will interact with connected devices nearly 4,800 times per day—basically one interaction every 18 seconds."[1]

Dr. Janusz Bryzek, vice president of MEMS and sensing solutions at Fairchild Semiconductor, predicts there will be 45 trillion networked sensors 20 years from now. This will be driven by smart systems, including IoT, mobile and wearable market growth, digital health, context computing, global environmental monitoring, and artificial intelligence (AI), hyper imaging, macroscopes, medical "labs on a chip," and silicon photonics IoT is conjoined with the Internet of Everything.[2]

IoT is having an impact on many industry verticals, including supply chain and retail, communications, medical and health care, building and construction (smart buildings), waste management in the environment, water resources, industrial applications, energy (smart grid), transportation, and education (learning analytics).

Where do AI and the IoT go from here? Wearables, smart homes, smart cities, and smart industries are the four main areas where AIoT (the combination of AI and IoT) is having an impact.

- ◆ **Wearables.** Smartwatches and other wearables are examples of devices that continuously track and monitor user preferences and behaviors. This has resulted in useful applications not only for the health tech industry but also for sports and fitness. Leading IT research firm Gartner predicts that by 2023, the worldwide wearable device market will generate more than $87 billion in sales.
- ◆ **Smart homes.** Science fiction is no longer the only genre that has houses that can fulfill all of your requests. Using appliances, lighting, electronics, and other resources, smart houses can learn about their homeowners' behaviors and provide automated support.

  Improved energy efficiency has additional benefits that come with this easy access. Therefore, it is possible that the smart home industry would expand at a compound annual growth rate of 25% from 2020 to 2025, when it is expected to reach $246 billion.

◆ **Smart cities.** Cities are becoming safer and more convenient places to live as an increasing number of people move from rural to urban areas. With funds flowing toward enhancing energy efficiency, transportation, and public safety, smart city solutions are being tested and adopted.

AI's useful uses in traffic control are already starting to become apparent. Real-time dynamic decisions on traffic flows are made by an Intelligent Transport Management System in New Delhi, which has some of the most crowded roadways in the world.

◆ **Smart industries.** The digital transformation of industries like mining and manufacturing helps them become more productive and less prone to human mistakes.

Smart gadgets, such as supply chain sensors and real-time data analytics, help businesses avoid expensive mistakes.[3]

Attack Vulnerability of the Internet of Things

There are many different kinds of IoT devices, and safeguarding such as a broad target for attack is a challenging endeavor, particularly given the variety of device types and security protocols. The general belief is that anything connected can be compromised when it comes to security operations on these billions of IoT devices.

In light of the growing prevalence of IoT assaults, particularly when teleworking and remote office trends are considered, recognizing and comprehending the hazard is crucial. Every IoT device is an attack surface that might provide hackers with access to your data.

IoT gadgets also present particular difficulties. In contrast to laptops and smartphones, the majority of IoT devices have lower processing and storage capacities. It is therefore challenging to use firewalls, antivirus software, and other security tools that could aid in their protection. In addition, edge computing cleverly gathers nearby data, which concentrates threats for more experienced players.

The emergence of edge computing, a term used to describe our linked society, can be attributed to the IoT. Near the point of data creation, edge computing delivers analytics and processing capacity. To optimize processing speeds and minimize bandwidth needs, edge computing catalyzes the transition to data-driven edge infrastructure. Safely storing, prioritizing, analyzing, exchanging, and scaling device data are essential for operations and commerce. To minimize latency, edge computing seeks to shift data storage, real-time processing, and activities away from a central location and closer to the device itself.

The past decade has recorded many botnet cyberattacks that have affected the IoT. One example is the massive and high-profile Mirai botnet DDoS attack in 2016. Mirai was an IoT botnet made up of hundreds of thousands of compromised IoT devices. It targeted Dyn—a domain name system provider for many well-known internet platforms in a distributed denial-of-service (DDoS) attack. That DDoS attack sent millions of bytes of traffic to a single server to cause the system to shut down. The Dyn attacks leveraged IoT devices and some of the attacks were launched by common devices like digital routers, webcams, and video recorders infected with malware.

In March 2021, a cyberattack occurred on the cloud-based video surveillance service Verkada. Using authentic admin account credentials that could be available online, the attackers were able to access the private data of Verkada software clients as well as live feeds from over 150,000 cameras installed in factories, hospitals, schools, jails, and other locations.

It was eventually discovered that more than 100 workers had "super admin" access, giving them access to thousands of customer cameras. This highlighted the dangers of having too many privileged users.[4]

In 2018, a large botnet victimized the GitHub software development platform in one of the largest DDoS attacks ever recorded. That attack took the platform offline. There have been many other alarming high-profile IoT botnet attacks in the past few years. You can find a good historical list of botnet attacks at this link: https://netacea .com/glossary/list-of-botnets/.

Standard and Regulations for IoT

An IoT system failure can result in serious issues for computer networks and sensitive data because IoT entails connecting various devices and storing a lot of data. Consequently, there are many legal and regulatory issues to consider.

The lack of a single manufacturer standard or regulation regarding security is a significant liability of IoT. Consequently, you are receiving products that are assembled after having been made in various parts of the world, and they typically lack adequate security. Individuals usually do not alter their gadgets' default passwords.

Recently, the United States Government Accountability Office (GAO) issued an assessment of the status of and security issues surrounding the IoT. The GAO identified the following types of attacks as primary threats to IoT:[5]

- Denial of service
- Malware
- Passive wiretapping
- Structured query language injection (SQLi controls a web application's database server)
- Wardriving (search for Wi-Fi networks by a person in a moving vehicle)
- Zero-day exploits

Knowing the threats and how to mitigate them is key. But the proliferation and rapid technological advancement of IoT devices pose noteworthy regulatory obstacles. Complying with regulations is made more difficult by the global nature of IoT. The data that IoT devices collect may be processed and stored in multiple nations, and these devices frequently travel across national borders.

Regulation necessitates a thoughtful strategy that considers consumer protection, international coordination, privacy, and security. A concerted worldwide regulatory response is required against that backdrop.

Smart Cities

As a part of the IoT world, smart cities are being constructed. The phrase *smart city* refers to the development of a public-private infrastructure for the purpose of conducting citizen security and protection operations. A wide range of systems, including emergency management systems, streetlights, smart power meters, water resource monitoring, waste management, smart building technologies, and security services are all integrated into the concept of smart cities. It is a convergence of physical and cyber systems.

For technologists, creating smart cities is an absolute requirement rather than an idealistic endeavor. They believe that smart cities will be the future. And according to World Bank forecasts, the percentage of people living in urban areas worldwide will increase from 56% to 70% by 2050.[6]

In any smart city, cyber safety and security are critical. The safe networking of embedded sensors is essential to the operations and services provided by smart cities. Like any other digitally connected equipment, these sensors are susceptible to corruption and hacking; therefore robust cybersecurity software, hardware, and protocols are needed.

These sensors can offer better situational and conditional awareness wherever they are placed, enabling communication and information sharing between residents and first responders. The success of smart cities lies in their acceptance and integration into the community and their ability to automate communication to alert and/or locate people in case of location-based emergencies that leverage the association between a handheld mobile device and a wireless network. The capability enables faster responses to medical emergencies, natural disasters, or in response to crimes.

Our vulnerability will increase as we become increasingly digitally connected in our personal and professional lives. The need to mitigate cyber dangers will only increase, necessitating data security and reliability. On the IoT, smart cities, and with our own mobile smartphones that sit at the edge of the internet, the same components of vigilance, preparedness, and resilience need to be applied to a personal as well as business settings. Figure 20.1 shows the attack surfaces and vulnerabilities of the IoT.

Understanding what gadgets are connected in the IoT environment, knowing how to safeguard the most valuable assets, and successfully resolving security events and breaches are the main components of the IoT security issues.

The combination of AI's machine learning models with IoT's data sharing and connectivity capabilities would enable AI to analyze the data that IoT systems gather. This would be the main area

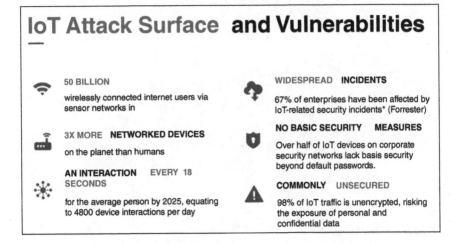

Figure 20.1   IoT attack surfaces and vulnerabilities.

Source: Raut, Niket. (2021, March 3). A converged approach to IOT cybersecurity. Capgemini. https://www.capgemini.com/insights/expert-perspectives/a-converged-approach-to-iot-cybersecurity/

of synergy between the two technologies. IoT devices would be able to comprehend and analyze data instead of just collecting and sending it, resulting in much improved operations, by integrating AI. AI has the potential to identify security flaws in networked devices and offer real-time monitoring to prevent breaches.

CHAPTER 20

5G

With faster speeds, greater capacity, and improved dependability, the move into 5G networks offers encouraging advantages for its end users in preparation for the widespread deployment of the Internet of Things (IoT).

Similar to existing wireless networks, 5G depends on cells in order to operate. A 5G antennae and base station bounce radio waves that connect a wireless device, like a phone, laptop, or tablet, to the internet within each cell. 5G is powered by the same technology as all of the preceding wireless network generations; however, there are significant differences from earlier networks.

Cellular technology has advanced to a new level with fifth-generation wireless (5G). By lowering latency (lack of responsiveness) in comparison to earlier wireless standards, 5G was designed to significantly boost the speed and bandwidth of wireless networks. Data transmission speeds and encoding techniques of each iteration of cellular technology vary, necessitating device upgrades for end users.

For enterprises, 5G is already providing quicker networks with greater capacity and reduced latency or lag times. The US economy and the enterprise business community will reap countless benefits from 5G. Wireless and advanced 5G networks will offer many advantages, such as greater dependability and traffic capacity. When it is fully integrated, 5G will operate like a superhighway for data. Millions will benefit from broadband connectivity. It will also enable real-time processing and analytics, which will have an influence on

159

commercial verticals like retail, health, and finance, in addition to greater traffic capacities, reduced latency, and enhanced reliability.

In populated urban areas where automobile and foot traffic have long caused gridlock and pollution of the air and noise, cities are already using 5G to help with traffic flow and air quality through sensors connected to the IoT, but much more innovation in this field is expected in the future. Smart cities have a lot of opportunities to take advantage of 5G's artificial intelligence (AI) capabilities. Tests are underway for applications that would use 5G-enabled AI to help with everything from better energy management to 911 call routing.

Cloud computing, where AI needs a lot of processing capacity to manage the data it is tasked with analyzing, is one area where edge computing is especially well positioned for growth. In this case, achieving value for the business depends on 5G connectivity and dependability.

Real-time AI analysis of massive amounts of data for applications ranging from health and fitness to remotely operated vehicles like satellites and drones might become possible very soon thanks to edge computing. Considering its potential, enterprise data processing is rapidly moving toward standardizing on 5G-enabled edge computing. It is also seeing new adoptions in industries such as health care and finance.

In California, the Palo Alto VA Medical Center provided an example of the benefits of using 5G applications. Having recently become the first hospital in the nation to be fully 5G ready, the facility is now able to transfer massive volumes of data and implement innovative patient technologies, such as displaying MRI or X-ray pictures onto a patient's body as part of preoperative planning.[1]

When communication is critical and time critical, emergency responders rely on 5G to provide prompt, dependable, and efficient service. In the case of a fire or tunnel collapse during mining operations, communication delays underground might be disastrous.

Losing power or the capacity to transmit data can destroy transactional data in retail or financial services systems, which can cause a financial catastrophe. The possible loss of confidence and financial liability from network failures is simply too great for banks handling transactions worth millions of dollars.

In order to manage traffic and improve safety and efficiency of travel, autonomous cars will need to depend on intelligent roadways. Law enforcement agencies and municipal fleets will be monitored by governments through 5G apps. To maintain agricultural yields and improve irrigation, autonomous farming will make use of robotic equipment. Robotic decision-making that is fluid and quick will be the backbone of smart factories and warehouses, affecting logistics and production.

The increased speed, performance, capacity, and connectivity of 5G will make increased security necessary. Like any modern technology, there are security risks with 5G. Due to the highly sensitive political context of 5G's supply chain roots and controls coming from China, several of these cybersecurity-related issues have been brought up in security talks among the US intelligence and national security establishments in the United States and Europe.

There are also serious vulnerabilities associated with the larger attack surface that 5G will provide. An ecosystem of 5G network–connected devices, applications, and services, ranging from drones and autonomous cars to smart factories and mobile phones, will increase the number of entry points for hackers.

Due to the fact that 5G does not completely remove security issues, it is crucial to regularly update and patch all operating systems and other cybersecurity tools to ensure that the majority of security holes are fixed. This includes laptops, iPads, iPhones, and other smart personal devices, not just network tools.

5G will make data move faster, which could be a problem if someone is trying to do harm. Do two things to get a better idea of possible data leak problems: (1) Find out where your data regularly goes, like the cloud; this will help you understand "normal activity" in terms of both location and amount when you look at your logs. (2) Find out where your data shouldn't be going and what amounts of data in transit are normal or not normal. Accurate and quick log review will still be necessary in a 5G setting.

With the huge increase in internet traffic and the recent improvements in 5G speed, it is important to check if your network has enough staff or bandwidth to spot any strange behavior. By looking into machine learning solutions that can automatically spot strange network activity and confirm an employee's permission to access the network (for example, identity and access management is a set of rules, procedures, and tools for controlling user access to important data), this can be done.

It is problematic that broad deployment has been delayed in many countries by slower-than-expected infrastructure upgrades, economic downturns, political problems, and practical issues like long distances that require the installation of more small cells to support 5G's shorter wavelengths. Today's smartphones say they can connect to 5G networks, but fewer than half of wireless users can actually connect to these networks.

Although, that number will change over the next few years as more infrastructure is built. Future work on 5G networks is likely to continue. Stable power and infrastructure solutions will be very important for the success and wide use of 5G network features.

CHAPTER 21

Quantum Computing

Since the 1960s, when the electronic calculator was invented, the field of computing has seen tremendous breakthroughs. Thanks to technology, things that were formerly considered science fiction dreams are now reality. Our processing equipment is getting smaller and more versatile, while classical computing has become enormously quicker and more capable.

Quantum computing, like artificial intelligence (AI), will create a technological paradigm shift for humankind. Computing of the future will be guided by artificial synapses that resemble those of the human brain. The components could be based on transistors, chemicals, biological, photonics, or quantum components, and they could be either analog or digital. The transition from classical computing to quantum computing has already begun. Quantum computing has the power to transform industries, spur scientific advancement, and catalyze innovation in the digital age by using the concepts of quantum physics to execute computations at a scale never seen before.

Quantum computing is defined by the research firm Gartner as "the use of atomic quantum states to effect computation." Quantum bits, or qubits, store data and are capable of holding all states concurrently and can represent a range of values in one qubit, rather than the more conventional binary bits of ones and zeros. This representation is called *superpositioning*.

Superpositioning is what gives quantum computers speed and parallelism (quantum parallelism is when quantum systems can explore and process multiple computational paths simultaneously), because each qubit can represent a quantitative solution to a problem. Further, qubits can be linked with other qubits in a process called *entanglement*; each entangled qubit adds two more dimensions to the system. When combined with superposition, quantum computers can process a massive number of possible outcomes at the same time.[1]

According to *Scientific American*, "Quantum computers rely on the same physical rules as atoms to manipulate information." In the same way that conventional computers operate software programs through logical circuits, quantum computers operate quantum circuits through the principles of superposition, entanglement, and interference in physics.[2]

Scientists are working on creating quantum computers, which would allow for completely new forms of cryptography, analytics, and calculations at incredibly fast speeds. Within the quantum domain, photonics computers—which transport and process data using light photons rather than electrons—are also being created.

The speed and power of quantum computing will enable us to address some of the most significant and difficult problems facing humanity. For example, in an effort to improve the batteries used in its electric vehicles, Mercedes-Benz is investigating quantum computing. By integrating quantum computing into its products, the company hopes to affect the environment and define the future of modern electrically driven automobiles, all while working toward becoming carbon neutral by 2039. Even with today's most sophisticated computers, simulating the behavior of batteries is a very challenging task. Mercedes-Benz, however, can replicate the chemical reactions in automobile batteries more precisely by using quantum computing technology.

Another example is ExxonMobil, who is using quantum algorithms to make it easier to find the best routes for shipping clean-burning fuel throughout the globe. Completing all of the routing calculations would be impossible without quantum computing.[3]

When combined with AI, research, learning, and predictive analytics will all undergo paradigm shifts in society. With the integration of AI and data analytics, quantum computing is expected to transform the landscape and propel humanity's ability to answer challenges faster than ever before. According to futurist Ray Kurzweil, processing power doubles every two years on average, and humanity will be able to "expand the scope of our intelligence a billion-fold."[4]

According to *The Quantum Insider*, new developments are putting quantum computing closer to reality by making it more efficient to scale and easier to build.

Scientists from Simon Fraser University have released a study in *Nature* that they say could lead to an all-silicon quantum internet and quantum computers that can solve real-world computer problems. In theory, that internet will be a lot safer and faster than the one we use now.

In the study, the scientists describe their observations of silicon 'T centre' photon-spin qubits, an important milestone that unlocks immediate opportunities to construct massively scalable quantum computers and the quantum internet that will connect them.[5]

AI combined with quantum computing will revolutionize our future. AI processes and analyzes enormous data sets primarily through the use of computer power. With its higher processing ability, quantum computing can expedite this process. More intricate and sophisticated AI models might be able to cut the time required for algorithms to compute from weeks to mere seconds.

It is envisioned by many that advances in quantum computing power and speed will help us solve some of the largest and most complex challenges we face as a civilization. Any science (e.g., physics, chemistry, mathematics, and biology) or industry (e.g., health care, finance, commerce, communications, security, cybersecurity and cryptography, energy, and space exploration) that relies on data will be affected by quantum computing abilities.

AI introduces new powers and alters existing ones, making it distinct from other technological waves. No technological wave has yet witnessed the raw expansion of power like that of quantum computing. This new wave of technology is all about doing, whereas previous major waves—that of computers and the internet—were about disseminating knowledge. Individuals' capabilities are about to undergo a radical shift at a rate that was unimaginable a few years ago.[6]

To put it plainly, we do not yet fully understand the technological consequences of quantum technologies and AI. Nothing we have ever experienced in the past can prepare us for what lies ahead.

CHAPTER 22

Quantum Technologies and Cybersecurity

Booz Allen Hamilton analysts predicted in 2021 that China will overtake the United States and Europe in quantum research and development and that Chinese hackers may soon target highly encrypted data sets, such as information about undercover intelligence officers or weapon designs, with the goal of decrypting them later on when quantum computing allows for it.

"Encrypted data with intelligence longevity, like biometric markers, covert intelligence officer and source identities, Social Security numbers, and weapons' designs, may be increasingly stolen under the expectation that they can eventually be decrypted," according to a BAH report titled "Chinese threats in the quantum era." "State-aligned cyber threat actors," according to the report, will begin to intercept or pilfer previously unusable encrypted data. The report warns that China may hack data for quantum decryption in the future.[1]

As the *Financial Times* reported, Chinese researchers assert that they have broken RSA encryption with a quantum computer—a claim that, if verified, would be years ahead of the anticipated arrival of such a capability. Even though the Chinese claims have not been verified (if they ever will be), they highlight the fact that quantum research is working hard toward that objective and that predictions about when RSA encryption will be broken might be more optimistic than realistic.[2]

Chief experience officer Tim Callan of cybersecurity start-up Sectigo recently told the *Daily Mail* that one day, already-existing quantum computers would "make the encryption we use today no longer fit for purpose. The development of quantum computers poses a serious threat to data security," he said. "Their enormous processing power can quickly crack encryption, leaving sensitive data—from bank account information to medical records to state secrets—vulnerable." This possibility is so alarming, according to him, that experts call it the *quantum apocalypse*. Finding the prime factors of a number is possible with Shor's algorithm, which is a quantum algorithm. An American scientist named Peter Shor came up with it in 1994.

The algorithm might be used by massive quantum computers to break any public key system based on integer factorization–based (or other) cryptography, which has led quantum researchers to also refer to this occasion as *Q-Day*.[3]

I spoke on the urgency of a Q-Day or quantum apocalypse in my talk, "A Look into Commercialising Quantum 2022 in London," at *The Economist* conference. Quantum computers, if placed in the wrong hands, have the potential to constitute geopolitical threats due to their superior speed and accuracy over classical computers. Additionally, the same computational power that makes it possible to tackle complicated problems can also be used to compromise cybersecurity. This is because current cybersecurity protocols usually encrypt sensitive data, like passwords and personal information, using pseudo-random numbers. However, quantum computers can break the techniques used by traditional computers to generate random numbers, which poses a serious risk to any organization that uses standard encryption tools. Figure 22.1 shows my quote from the conference.

"Security in the Quantum Era" is the title of a report published by the IBM Institute for Business Value. The necessity of "enterprise adoption of quantum-safe capabilities to safeguard the integrity of critical applications and infrastructure as the risk of decryption increases" is discussed in the paper along with the reality of quantum risk.

The IBM report also notes that cybercriminals may already be exfiltrating encrypted data with the goal of decrypting it once quantum computers advance as part of "harvest now, decrypt later attacks,"

Figure 22.1 Conference quote.
Source: Commercialising Quantum 2022 ECONOMIST IMPACT.

and it states that quantum computing poses an "existential risk" to classical computer encryption protocols.[4]

Considering that the decryption threat has been identified, my personal recommendation is to prepare now for the inevitable arrival of quantum computing, which is why it is imperative that governments, enterprises, and organizations safeguard their data. The good news is that we do not need to wait for technological advancements to address these issues because defense-related capabilities are already available on the market and quantum technology is capable of combating these threats. For further information, please read my article in *Forbes* titled "The Quantum Era Is Arriving, and It Will Be Transformational!"[5]

Quantum Computing Is Already Here in Some Forms

There are a variety of solutions coming together in quantum tech. Leading the way is full-stack quantum solutions. A company called Quantum Computing Inc. (QCI) (NASDAQ:QUBT) aims to speed up the supply of quantum information processing hardware devices that offer cybersecurity and performance advantages. The corporation is moving toward replacing classical type computing with entropy quantum computing using their current quantum photonics technology offerings, strengthening key sources for any cryptographic task.

In order to develop a core quantum photonics technology that can be implemented at room temperature in typical server room settings, Quantum Computing Inc. uses a quantum photonic system (QPS) to make use of pure, nonlinear optical features. They have already shown that their QPS systems and methods can produce highly precise computations for solving challenging business optimization problems, powerful single-photon measurements for remote sensing applications like Lidar, and 3D quantum imaging capabilities using radiation that is safe for human eyes in the visible and near infrared ranges.

With full connectivity between variables (high density), QCI's Entropy Quantum Computer (EQC) technology is specifically designed to tackle real-world optimization issues at a scale of 11,000 qubits. This pales in comparison to the more common small-scale issues that alternative quantum systems employ. In summary, the current EQC yields data that will enable industry to grow more quickly as this new quantum photonic technology develops.

Additionally, its entropy quantum computer has exceptionally low size, weight, power, and cost parameters and runs at low power levels (less than 80 watts). Its small, compact design enables it to fit in rack mounted or tabletop arrangements. No quantum specialists are needed to maintain and calibrate it.

"Photonics can also be leveraged to provide Quantum Encryption + Quantum Authentication on the same platform and is a full solution to replace public-private key cryptography that is vulnerable to evolving quantum threats," claims Robert Liscouski, CEO of Quantum Computing Inc.[6]

The Quantum Private Communication methodology patent from QCI offers a pure hardware solution that does not rely on pseudo-random numbers, algorithms, or mathematics, and it solves the issues with key distribution techniques that include trusted third-party authentication and validation. In a trustless system approach, patented methods using entangled photons and correlated true quantum random numbers produced from the quantum entropy source are coupled to provide a methodology that guarantees that only intended recipients of the information are properly certified.

Mr. Liscouski points out that the vulnerability of public key cryptography to an attack by Shor's algorithm could affect vital infrastructure, banking and financial systems, health care, and transportation. Using QPS, that threat is lessened for both near-term quantum systems and currently available classical systems. The company's technologies include a new photonic physically unclonable function chip that gives the user a unique authentication "quantum fingerprint" and a quantum random number generator.

This quantum photonic technology is welcome at a time when the West is engaged in a quantum computing supremacy race, particularly with China, which has the potential to drastically alter the global geopolitical landscape.

Chinese researchers revealed last year that they had broken the previous record of 18 km (11 miles) by setting a new world record for quantum secure direct communication at 102.2 km (64 miles). China has lately reported some astounding breakthroughs regarding its quantum communications capabilities. According to Engadget, researchers have broken the global record for quantum-encrypted communications. The Chinese are making significant investments in all fields of quantum research—estimated to be in the billions of dollars—and they are showing results.

The quantity of money invested in the United States, Europe, and with partners in Asia is also increasing. The Japanese government joined the global race in quantum computing by deploying its first homegrown quantum computer in 2023.[7] "The government strategy aims to create an environment where quantum technology can be used in such varied fields as medicine, banking, and new materials development by 2030, with a target of 10 million users in Japan."[8]

In order to get ready for a Q-Day, the US government has mandated new quantum proof criteria for algorithms. Quantum-resistant, or post-quantum, encryption is seen by the National Security Agency (NSA) as a more practical and affordable option than quantum key distribution. For all of these reasons, the NSA/Central Security Service's Cybersecurity section does not endorse the use of quantum key distribution (QKD) or quantum cryptography (QC) to secure communications in any NSS systems, nor does it plan to certify or approve any QKD or QC security products for use by NSS users. The moment is ideal for testing and implementing QCI's Quantum Private Communication Network and other post-quantum technology applications in a zero trust setting.

Legislative priorities now include preventing the threat of enemies decrypting sensitive information taken from agencies, businesses, networks, and data centers. Congress enacted the Quantum Computing Cybersecurity Preparedness Act in December 2022. "To prioritize the migration of federal information technology systems to post-quantum cryptography and come up with guidance for the federal assessment of critical systems based on the standards that the National Institute of Standards and Technology will issue for post-quantum cryptography," is what the legislation instructs the Office of Management and Budget to do. This is a positive move because it forces us to consider the security consequences of not being prepared for our quantum age.

The quantum computing players are not limited to governments. The industry is actively investing in quantum capabilities and techniques, with companies such as Intel, Google, IBM, D-Wave, and others. Additionally, academia is becoming more active with quantum. Researchers at the University of Chicago's Pritzker School of Molecular Engineering, home of the Chicago Quantum Exchange (CQE), recently reported a significant advancement: they have established a quantum network that connects suburban labs and the city of Chicago. The Chicago network, one of the first publicly accessible testbeds for quantum security technology in the country, will be made available to academia and industry. Chicago Quantum Exchange is growing and energizing its quantum network, moving closer to a secure quantum internet.

For further information on quantum advances, two prestigious universities to keep an eye on are the Massachusetts Institute of Technology and the University of Chicago. Additionally, two excellent sites for researchers are IEEE Quantum (https://quantum.ieee.org/) and the Quantum Security Alliance (http://www.quantumsecurityalliance .org/), which bring together industry, academia, and US government agencies to discover, define, and work together on technological advancements in quantum computing.

CHAPTER 23

Quantum Internet of Things

Another "entanglement" with quantum has to do with how it interacts with the Internet of Things (IoT), which encompasses items that can be read, recognized, located, addressed, and/or controlled through the internet. It includes all of the following: people, machines, data, sensors, devices, and their interactions. According to an estimate by Business Insider, 40 billion IoT devices were installed globally by corporations, governments, and consumers in 2023.[1]

As the IoT and the new digital economy continue to develop quickly, edge devices and data are multiplying at astounding rates. The current issue is how to keep an eye on and guarantee the IoT provides high-quality services. Efficiency, scalability, procedures, and responsiveness are necessary for any breakthrough technology or capacity to function as intended, in particular over trillions of sensors.

Quantum technologies will specifically affect the following areas: enhanced storage and data memory capacity, safe cloud computing, virtualization, artificial intelligence (AI) (human/computer and machine/computer interfaces), network latency, interoperability, and the developing 5G telecommunications infrastructure. Safe end-to-end communications are essential for 5G, and quantum encryption, which creates safe codes, might be the answer to the fast-expanding IoT.

IoT security is a critical concern. Cryptographic methods are currently employed on the IoT to aid secure communication (validation and verification). However, because they use public key systems, in the not too distant future skilled hackers with quantum computers might be able to crack their encryption.

Without a doubt, quantum technology—particularly quantum computing—has enormous promise to transform a wide range of industries, including communications, real-time data analytics, biotechnology, genetic sequencing, and materials research. By affecting the field of AI and the metaverse, quantum computing will also hasten the future. However, in addition to the good, we also need to prepare ahead and stop the bad—most important, data, which is essential to economies and trade. It is crucial to take a quantum-proof cybersecurity path from the beginning.

A recent study titled "Quantum Computing Market & Technologies 2018–2024" provides a glimpse into our quantum future:

> We are in the midst of a "Quantum Computing Supremacy Race," one that will result in groundbreaking computing power that surpasses the performance of digital supercomputers. The quantum computing technologies have the potential to change long-held dynamics in commerce, intelligence, military affairs, and strategic balance of power.
>
> Advances in quantum computer design, fault-tolerant algorithms, and new fabrication technologies are now transforming this "holy grail" technology into a realistic program poised to surpass traditional computation in some applications. With these new developments, the key question that companies are asking is not whether there will be a quantum computer, but who will build it and benefit from it.[2]

A worthwhile summary of the fundamentals of quantum computing and its potential impact of various industries and scientific disciplines was provided by *DotCom Magazine*.[3] As stated in a report by the consulting company McKinsey & Company, the automobile, chemicals, financial services, and health sciences sectors are the four most likely to have an early economic impact from quantum computing. The study projected that by 2035, technology would have increased value in those four businesses by a total of $1.3 trillion.[4]

We are undoubtedly on the verge of a new era marked by quantum computing and the digital revolution, even though we are still in the midst of quantum research and discoveries. Although it is still in its infancy, we might get there sooner than we thought—in less than 10 years.

We must get ready for the exponential advantages and threats of quantum technology right away due to its potentially disruptive nature. More investment in R&D from the public and private sectors will be required as a result. Planning and implementation of quantum education and workforce development are also necessary for our rapidly approaching quantum future.

CHAPTER 24

The Holy Digital Grail
Cybersecurity Risk Management

A fundamental principle of cybersecurity is that it should be mission-relevant and easily integrated into the business. A complete security system that is multilayered and data-centric ought to be user-friendly, if not imperceptible. Data security cannot cause slowness or obstruct the average user's daily workflow given the demands of the goal. Data protection is essential to risk reduction for cybersecurity practitioners, and it should be integrated into the ecosystem by using the investments already made in security information and event management and data loss prevention.

Organizations can gain a strong audit position by implementing a complete data protection strategy that incorporates real-time data visibility down to users, devices, and geolocations, allowing for the knowledge of exactly where the data is, who is attempting to access it, and what they are doing.

In spite of the increasing frequency, sophistication, lethality, and liabilities linked to intrusions, industry management has lacked readiness and moved slowly to strengthen cybersecurity. Businesses must prioritize cybersecurity if they are to prosper in the complex and constantly evolving technological threat landscape of today. A sound risk management plan will identify digital assets and data that needs to be secured by creating a vulnerability framework. Through the rapid identification and prioritization of cyber vulnerabilities, a risk assessment can help you improve overall operational cybersecurity and promptly deploy solutions to safeguard vital assets from malevolent cyberattackers.

This strategy should include using new security solutions (encryption, threat intelligence and detection, and firewalls) and policies to safeguard and back up company enterprise systems, including financial systems, email exchange servers, HR, and procurement systems. It is also crucial to include AI into a thorough plan that incorporates cooperation, regulatory frameworks, and a cybersecurity-aware culture.

In the digital age, it makes sense for everyone to be proactive rather than reactive. To strengthen defenses and close gaps, a variety of tested cyber risk management techniques can be applied. All risk postures have one thing in common: avoid taking the chance of being complacent in the face of increasing cyberthreats and hazards.

The frequency and severity of cyberattacks (such as ransomware and distributed denial of service assaults against networks) are rising. Growing cyber threats to a company's operations, reputation, and intellectual property might affect not just stock prices but also the company's ability to stay in business. The threat of hacker-caused data breaches is growing, making cybersecurity a critical international concern. Gartner has forecasted that 60% of digital enterprises might experience significant losses as a result of their security teams' incapacity to handle digital hazards.[1]

A cyber vulnerability risk assessment is the basis of any commitment to cybersecurity. A crucial first step in following cybersecurity best practices is completing that action item. A risk assessment may swiftly locate and rank cyber vulnerabilities, enabling you to promptly implement countermeasures to safeguard important assets from malevolent actors online and enhance operational cybersecurity in general.

Application security testing should be the first step in that evaluation process in order to find any code vulnerabilities, configuration errors, or even malware that may already be present in programs and applications. Testing can also confirm compliance with external regulatory standards and required internal audits for state and municipal governance regulations.

Penetration testing and simulation are crucial for readiness. Everyone functioning in the new digital environment should start with testing, but businesses are particularly vulnerable to increasingly skilled hackers. Finding problems before they enter production and taint devices and networks is the main goal of the testing and validation testing procedure. However, it must be ongoing because platforms frequently add new code and threats change over time. Although new code poses a risk, many programs and apps can already be running on outdated systems with vulnerabilities and potential access points. Therefore, as part of vulnerability and validity testing, old code must also be assessed for patches along with any new code.

Companies should use simulation as a crucial component of their cybersecurity readiness in addition to penetration testing. Unfortunately, penetration examinations might miss exploits and are sometimes too expensive for small and medium-sized enterprises. Vulnerability scan and penetration test capabilities can be enhanced, and testing barriers reduced with the use of a process known as breach and attack simulation.

The efficacy of email filters, endpoint security, and web application firewalls can all be evaluated by conducting simulated attacks on the different security solutions that an organization has deployed. Tests can also verify whether security policies and controls are set up correctly, which is another major vulnerability that hackers exploit.

Artificial intelligence, machine intelligence, the Internet of Things, 5G, virtual and augmented reality, and quantum computing are just a few examples of the quickly evolving technological landscape that will drastically alter business operating models and security over the next 10 years.

There are many obstacles to overcome when operating securely in a digital world that is always changing due to new technological advancements. Many times, cybersecurity is misinterpreted and oversimplified. The world of cyber threats is multifaceted, intricate, and vulnerable to constantly changing threats from a range of actors using advanced hacking techniques.

Defined by the most basic elements in informed risk management, cybersecurity is composed of these elements:

- Layered vigilance (intelligence, surveillance)
- Readiness (operational capabilities, visual command center interdiction technologies)
- Resilience (coordinated incident response, mitigation, and recovery)

Those elements are best understood and used by constructing a risk management plan that addresses opportunities and gaps to fortify cybersecurity in an emerging tech era.

CHAPTER 25

The Urgency of Having a Cyber Risk Management Plan

The most effective cyber defense remains a complete risk management plan. A practical cybersecurity risk management for any organization will necessitate identifying risks and reorganizing its strategies to recognize, neutralize, and reduce emerging cyber threats.

Currently, the majority of cyber defense solutions typically include five stages of risk management components:

1. Determine which assets are most important.
2. Guard by restricting access.
3. Look for any breaches.
4. React to stop the intruder.
5. Recuperate by going back to your routine.

Including a strategy that reduces the time that criminals can stay in the system and limiting the exfiltration of data could provide another layer of security.

I created the following list based on the important categories found on many typical risk plans, including some of the overarching elements that should be considered in all cybersecurity frameworks:

◆ Carry out vulnerability assessments of all devices (including work-from-home devices) connected to governing networks.

- Carry out comprehensive scanning and testing to detect malware in code and configurations that can be exploited, especially with legacy systems.
- Use multilayered and in-depth cybersecurity protections including strong passwords, multifactor authentication, and strong endpoint protections. Encrypt sensitive assets, especially data in transit. Use firewalls, antivirus detection software, and continually audit networks.
- Back up all critical data and assets, especially data potentially targeted by ransomware.
- Create policies and visibility (secure routers, Wi-Fi) and remote work protocols for all work-from-home activities of employees.
- Update and patch vulnerabilities to networks and devices.
- Compartmentalize all devices to minimize attack surfaces. Consider adding security software, containers, and devices to digitally fence network and devices.
- Establish privileged access for state, local, tribal government (SLTG) networks device controls and applications. (Use authentication and biometrics for access control.)
- Ensure mobile device security and interoperability for law enforcement and first responders.
- Continually monitor and share cyber threat intelligence across jurisdictions (could be done via fusion centers).
- Implement cybersecurity hygiene and awareness training for employees. (This is essential because most breaches are the result of phishing attacks and/or negligence.)
- Create a cybersecurity incident response and communications plan, especially for ransomware attacks.
- Determine what is required for resilience in cyber incident response and disaster recovery planning while removing single points of failure.
- Consider augmenting efforts with managed security and outside subject matter experts.
- Consider cloud security as a service.
- Evaluate emerging cybersecurity artificial intelligence (AI) automation and machine learning (ML) technologies.
- Plan for compliance and regulatory requirements.

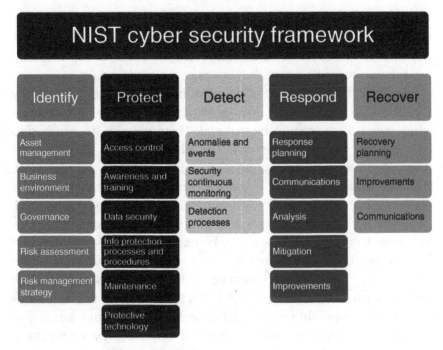

Figure 25.1 NIST cybersecurity framework.
Source: NIST. https://ioc.wiki/_media/wiki/nist-csf.png

The NIST Framework

The details of a security strategy can change depending on the scenario, but situational awareness and methodical skills for vital communications in an emergency are the threads that bind the pieces together. These guidelines are represented in the US government's National Institute of Standards and Technology (NIST) mantra for industry and government: "Identify, Protect, Detect, Respond, Recover" (see Figure 25.1).

New Securities Exchange Corporation Cybersecurity Regulations

A cybersecurity framework is even more important due to the adoption of new Securities and Exchange Commission (SEC) regulations that emphasize risk management for cybersecurity and impose penalties on businesses that fail to report breaches or recognize the significance of comprehending and mitigating growing cyber threats. Companies are now required by the SEC's new cyber disclosure rule to provide investors with up-to-date, consistent, and "decision-useful" information regarding how they manage their cyber risks.

According to the latest SEC regulations, registrants (any company that files with the SEC) will now be required to disclose any cybersecurity event they deem to be material. They will also be required to characterize the incident's material characteristics, including its nature, breadth, and timing, as well as its impact on the registrant. Four business days after a registrant concludes that a cybersecurity event is substantial, an Item 1.05 Form 8-K is required to be submitted.

"Whether a company loses a factory in a fire—or millions of files in a cybersecurity incident—it may be material to investors," said SEC Chair Gary Gensler. "Currently, many public companies provide cybersecurity disclosure to investors. I think companies and investors alike, however, would benefit if this disclosure were made in a more consistent, comparable, and decision-useful way. Through helping to ensure that companies disclose material cybersecurity information, today's rules will benefit investors, companies, and the markets connecting them."[1]

Risk Management Pillars for the New Technological Era

Because of the impact of technology on risk, old models for risk management can become quickly obsolete. It is important to view risk from a different perspective as we evolve in the current technological era.

Every organization must be adept at risk management, including risk exposure, to comply with SEC regulations. This goes beyond having a general understanding of the many threats and perils. Depending on your requirements and the degree of threat, you should evaluate several complete risk management security techniques (what I call the *three pillars*):

- ♦ **Security by design.** When it comes to risk management, security by design is actually the first step—especially for software or hardware developers who are worried about security. According to a recent analysis by the Cybersecurity and

Infrastructure Security Agency (CISA), security by design "means that technology products are built in a way that reasonably protects against malicious cyber actors successfully gaining access to devices, data, and connected infrastructure."[2]

As per CISA, technological goods that are secure by design are constructed in a way that inherently hinders malevolent cyber actors from effectively obtaining access to data, infrastructure, and networked devices. Software developers should also do a risk assessment to determine the most common cyberthreats to critical systems, according to CISA. Then, they should incorporate security measures into their designs, taking into consideration the ever-changing cyber threat landscape.

To stop adversary acts from breaching systems or gaining unauthorized access to sensitive data, it is also advised to use defense in depth, or several levels of security, in conjunction with secure information technology (IT) development standards.

◆ **Defense in depth.** Defense in depth offers an extra method of risk control and has multiple definitions in the security community. According to a NIST article, the defense in depth concept is "an important security architecture principle that has significant application to industrial control systems, cloud services, storehouses of sensitive data, and many other areas." We believe that a defense in depth strategy that is both "deep," indicating several levels of security, and "narrow," indicating fewer node-independent attack paths, is ideal.[3]

◆ **Zero trust.** An additional cornerstone of cybersecurity risk management is zero trust, which is a method where access to data, networks, and infrastructure is limited to what is necessary and where the validity of that access needs to be continuously confirmed.

Executive Order 14028, "Improving the Nation's Cybersecurity," was released by the White House on May 12, 2021, in response to the government's recognition of this harmful trend. The order required agencies to implement zero trust frameworks and architecture to better safeguard their loopholes. The fundamental components of a zero trust architecture are to authenticate and authorize devices, users, and applications trying to access the network; to presume that everything in the network is potentially hostile; and to not base trust on the network's location.

More specifically, zero trust refers to a collection of evolving cybersecurity paradigms that place the focus of defenses not on static, network-based perimeters but rather on users, assets, and resources. According to the idea of zero trust, assets or user accounts are not implicitly trusted alone based on the location of the assets (local area networks versus the internet), their ownership status (personal or enterprise), or their network location.

The idea of zero trust was developed in response to developments in business networks, including bring your own device, remote users, and cloud-based resources that are not located inside an organization's network perimeter. Zero trust emphasizes identity access management and data resource (assets, services, processes, network accounts) protection over network segmentation because the network location is no longer the fundamental determinant in establishing a resource's security posture.

When security by design, defense in depth, and zero trust are combined, cybersecurity becomes stronger. Security by design monitors, manages, and maintains the security process. Defense in depth enables layers of redundant protective security measures to help deter data breaches. Zero trust focuses on protecting resources (assets, services, workflows, network accounts) through strict identity, and access management enforced by authentication and proper authorization cybersecurity risk management, used together, will help to discover vulnerabilities, reduce risks, and strengthen defenses against an eventual cyberattack, and they should all be included in a cybersecurity framework approach. Of course, using these cyber risk management pillars is not the only thing that involves many additional components and procedures. When they are combined, one develops a more comprehensive worldview that facilitates planning and adaptation.

Risk Management Strategies at the Organizational Level

An essential part of any company or organizational cybersecurity program should be risk management. Vigilance is required, as are personnel training, gap identification, vulnerability assessment, risk reduction, and maintaining current resilience and incident response plans on hand to manage crises.

The core of cybersecurity is also catalyzed by risk management, supported not only by technology but also by leadership and a knowledgeable and up-to-date information security staff. There will always be security gaps, but with planning and cooperation, the dangers to systems can be decreased.

Although every company has its own culture, goals, and competencies, staff and management—including board members—are in charge of overseeing the business's cybersecurity-related operations. It should be everyone's responsibility to make sure that cybersecurity is the organization's top concern.

Effective communication is essential to achieving that objective and forms a fundamental component of cybersecurity. The chief technology officer, chief information officer, and chief information security officer, along with executive management, need to collaborate, coordinate, and regularly assess their network security, information security policies, and processes. Communication helps with readiness by facilitating the sharing of threat intelligence as well as new policies and technology that may have an impact on the cyber ecosystem.

It is important to understand the new SEC regulations. Ideally, a corporate board should include subject matter experts from both inside and outside the company. The views and recommendations of outside professionals are always beneficial to executive management. It helps avoid a state of complacency. There should be staff with specialized knowledge in governance, policy, liability insurance, cybersecurity technology solutions and services, training, and legal compliance.

Information security management should involve people who are experienced with the ISO 27001, the leading information security standard, and who are aware of best practices. To create sensible policy proposals, there must be strong links between the government and the business community. Public-private cooperation on sharing information about risks is encouraged by the Cybersecurity Information Exchange Act, especially when working with the Department of Homeland Security.

Despite cybersecurity investments, numerous firms, organizations, and authorities have experienced ongoing breaches throughout the years. Brand-new, highly advanced physical security and cybersecurity problems are now evolving and being deployed (including automated hacking tools) that seriously endanger persons, property, and business networks. Terrorists, criminals, hackers, organized crime, malevolent individuals, and in certain situations, hostile nation governments are among the evil global threat players.

To successfully fight rising cyber threats in 2024 and beyond, we need a risk management framework that is complete, flexible, and raised to the level of C-suite decision-making. We also need people to be more aware of and able to measure risk.

All-Inclusive Approach to Risk Management

Fundamentally, a risk management approach consists of gap identification, vulnerability assessment, and threat mitigation. Protecting key applications and guaranteeing data privacy should be the goals of an all-encompassing risk management strategy. Transparency is necessary to know the precise location of the data, as well as who is attempting to access it and what they are doing.

Every thorough risk management strategy should guarantee data privacy and safeguard critical applications. This calls for openness and understanding the precise location of the data, the identities of those attempting to access it, and their actions. Companies and organizations need to construct fortifications around the data once they have determined what needs to be protected. Any security approach that protects user data must be dynamic, not static. A solid risk management framework can continuously assess people, processes, and technological instruments that are used with any kind of data.

Automated cybersecurity tools for information assurance, resilience, and threat detection are the glue that will enable businesses to make the best use of emerging technology and run securely in a world where sensors and algorithms are convergent.

Tools to Help Enable Cyber Risk Management: Encryption and Cryptography

Various encryption techniques and standards are available based on the user's needs and specifications. The keys required for encrypted communication are generated and stored by hardware security modules that are customized. The ability to encrypt every data file with complete pervasive encryption is a more recent feature. With no changes to programs, full ubiquitous encryption enables you to completely encrypt data at the disk, database, and data set levels. This comprises a zero trust approach with several levels of thorough encryption, starting from the disk and moving up to the programs.

The majority of cybercriminals and hacktivists are thwarted by encryption because it places a significant time and effort barrier in their path. Data protection is becoming more and more important, regardless of where it is stored—on site, off site, in transit, or at rest. Encryption everywhere enables the safe integration of significant workloads and resilience in data recovery regardless of where the data is kept.

The government has mandated that data encryption be quantum-proof, and it is a crucial algorithmic aspect of security risk management. Applying a mathematical function to a file so that, without the decryption key, its contents are illegible and inaccessible is the general definition of encryption. Data encryption provides further security to the point of data use and shields consumers from compromised file records.

Additional components of cybersecurity architecture include cryptography. When using symmetric key encryption, the encrypted data is transferred and received by both computers using the same installed key. The secure sockets layer uses public key encryption (SSL). When sending sensitive data, internet servers and browsers frequently employ SSL.

Digital Conversion Tools

In the context of the Fourth Industrial Revolution's digital transformation, any security strategy for user data protection must be dynamic rather than static. Cyber threats will persist in changing as the attack surface and hacker sophistication increase. The majority of our essential infrastructures, such as those in the banking, energy, health care, and transportation sectors, function in a digital world. Risk management and the cybersecurity framework for businesses should prioritize and concentrate on these cybersecurity areas:

♦ **Endpoint security.** Safeguarding network access from a distance for a business
♦ **Network security.** Defending a network against assaults, unauthorized access, and invasions
♦ **Cloud security.** Guarding against unapproved users accessing a resource
♦ **Mobile security.** Defense against phony and dangerous applications
♦ **Cyberattacks on the supply chain.** Safeguarding every link in the chain
♦ **Data security and privacy regulations.** Protecting data and following privacy and data security guidelines
♦ **Identity management.** Comprehending each person's level of access within an organization
♦ **Business continuity/disaster recovery planning.** A well-thought-out strategy to keep the company running in the case of a breach

Cybersecurity Equals Economic Resilience

To sustain economic resilience, novel approaches to the development and application of vital and developing technologies, the cultivation of requisite human capital, and the establishment of confidence in the digital fabric that will intertwine our world are imperative. Integrating cybersecurity into a risk management framework is essential to that procedure.

Cybersecurity affects all types of enterprises, whether they are large or small, public, or private. IT may be used by any industry, including the legal, financial, retail, health care, entertainment, and energy sectors. Due to the prevalence of cyber threats and their potential to be catastrophic events for any organization, organizations

Cybersecurity Action List

Key Cyber Pursuits:
- Prioritize cybersecurity as a company imperative
- Create a risk management & vulnerability framework
- Obtain C-suite leadership and employee engagement
- Create incident mitigation and continuity plan

Identify Digital Assets to Be Protected:

Data (at rest and in motion)
- Network (firewalls, servers, routers, switches, WIFI)
- Devices (PC and mobile)
- Facilities
- People

Identify Top Cyber Threats:
- Malware (also polymorphic)
- Social engineering
- Phishing
- Ransomware
- Insider threats
- DDOS attacks
- Botnets

Recognize Evolving Challenges:
- AI enabled cyber attacks
- IoT – exponential connectivity
- Vulnerable supply chains
- Transition to cloud, hybrid cloud and edge platforms
- Quantum computing

Explore Remedies:
- Secure back-up protocols
- Cyber hygiene and strong passwords
- Access control
- Pen and vulnerability testing
- Encryption
- Antivirus software
- Threat intelligence
- New automated security tools
- Quick-response teams
- Incident response
- Red team, blue team, purple team

Explore Mitigation Strategies:
- Zero trust
- Security by design
- Defense in depth
- OT/ITConvergence

Figure 25.2   Cybersecurity action list.

must develop an operational cybersecurity risk management plan that is both operational and adaptive. I created the generic cybersecurity action list to assist in risk management planning (see Figure 25.2).

The Need for Government and Industry Cooperation

The establishment of public-private partnerships founded on risk management frameworks is a fundamental component of putting a security risk approach into practice. Increasingly, public-private cooperation is required to combat cyber threats. Leadership in the government and business must be prepared and committed. In order to build resiliency plans and make the best use of risk management models, industry and government should work together.

Sharing information about risks and dangers is one of the main purposes of industry and government cooperation. By exchanging this kind of information, industry and government can stay informed about the most recent ransomware, malware, phishing frauds, viruses, and insider threats. Sharing information also creates working procedures for resilience and lessons learned, which are essential for the success of trade and the prosecution of cybercrimes.

Protecting vital infrastructure requires minimizing changing risks and resisting intrusions. Information sharing, planning, investing in innovative technology, and the distribution of resources (and duties and responsibilities) across the public and private sectors in special working cybersecurity partnerships are all necessary for successful industry-government collaboration.

Cooperation is crucial for resolving cyberattacks as well. The Colonial pipeline breaches and SolarWinds both show how the government is helping to reduce breaches and increase resilience. In order to ascertain the scope of the violations and potential remedies, the government worked closely with the corporations.

The Joint Cyber Defense Collaborative (JCDC) was established by CISA, led by Jen Esterly, and last year radically altered the way that cyber risk is decreased by ongoing operational cooperation between the government and reliable business partners, bringing together cyber defenders from businesses across the globe. This multidisciplinary team proactively collects, evaluates, and disseminates relevant cyber risk data to facilitate coordinated, all-encompassing cybersecurity strategy, protection, and reaction. In collaboration with businesses, the JCDC receives support from other governmental organizations, such as the FBI, NSA, and US Cyber Command, to help reduce risk.[4]

It can be difficult to stay on top of cybersecurity concerns; public-private cooperation calls for a comprehensive approach. A major problem is adaptability and scalability to upgrade to new security technologies and processes given the broad range of architectures, systems, and jurisdictions.

The collaborative JCDC will also benefit cybersecurity research and development. Cybersecurity innovation will greatly benefit from cooperation between public and commercial players that involves information sharing and risk sharing. A sustainable, competitive bridge for the next generation of scientists and engineers to lead and achieve can also be created by combining funds and pipelines for R&D from the public and private sectors.

Enhanced information exchange, supply chain security, Internet of Things security tactics, managing the burgeoning 5G wireless infrastructure, employing AI and ML for cybersecurity defenses, and increasing workforce training to address the scarcity of qualified cybersecurity professionals are additional areas of focus.

Industry and government collaboration on information exchange and knowledge transfer, cybersecurity tool sharing, and occasionally pooling finance resources to develop prototypes and strengthen security-enhancing technology should be the cornerstones of a partnership.

Although many exciting and innovative technologies are being created, there is not a quick fix for cyber threat infiltration. However, several technologies show promise: enhanced encryption, biometric authentication, intelligent analytics, and automated network security. What can be improved through collaborative research, development, and deployment efforts includes informed risk management planning, training, network monitoring, and incorporating next-gen layered hardware/software technologies for the enterprise network, payload, and endpoint security.

In both the public and private sectors, technology foraging—or looking for clever ideas and technologies—is a crucial component of research and development. It provides the foundation for the development of novel goods, uses, and procedures that are introduced to the market. There are still a lot of undiscovered gems that need to be tapped into, marketed, licensed, and included in technological solutions. All breakthroughs in the developing technological spectrum, including those in cybersecurity, are benefited via foraging.

Governments and the corporate sector working together more closely could speed up the development of tactical and long-term strategic cybersecurity solutions. More investment needs be made in cooperative research and development to stay up-to-date with the constantly changing global danger matrix in fields like technology, software, and operational processes. There are no cybersecurity-related fields that do not require increased funding and upgrading to solve capability gaps.

The key to the advancement and use of AI is a genuine public-private partnership engine fueled by capital, creativity, and practical application. Naturally, accountability (security and trust) for the numerous emerging administrative, intellectual property, and ethical regulatory issues go hand-in-hand with disruptive technology.

In 2024 and beyond, cybersecurity policies should prioritize an improved and simplified relationship between the government and industry. Threats can change over time, particularly with the introduction of modern technologies like AI, ML, 5G, and eventually quantum computing.

Conclusion

Emerging Technologies, Cybersecurity, and Our Digital Future

We must impart knowledge to the next generation regarding the ramifications of the technologies discussed in this book and the potential for uneven effects on the future. Artificial intelligence (AI), the Internet of Things, 5G, and quantum tech are all fields where we might pursue parallel goals. We must comprehend the ethical and practical implications of transformative technologies because if we fail to do so, we will lose control over applications that can usurp the foundations of security and economic stability.

Enhanced and more capable next-gen cybersecurity tools and processes will be a core digital element that keeps us safe into the future. We must improve investments in technologies, processes, and people to be able to better mitigate the multitude of new sophisticated cyber threats on the horizon in our digitally fused ecosystems.

Though its potential must be used wisely and securely, AI can be a great ally in the fight against cyber threats. Navigating the obstacles and grabbing hold of the potential presented by this new digital frontier will require cooperative efforts from all parties.

AI is poised to revolutionize cybersecurity by providing security professionals with significant chances to enhance their assessment and reaction to threats. By automatically recognizing specific phishing attempts, for instance, AI copilots will assist in user defense.

Enterprises should put security first if they want to deploy AI successfully. This entails familiarizing yourself with your surroundings and data, balancing detection and prevention technologies, applying zero trust principles to safeguard data, and threat modeling to assess your risks. To get the most out of AI while lowering their security and privacy concerns, businesses should think about collaborating with reputable AI security companies.

Opportunities abound in the digital age. The current period, the Fourth Industrial Revolution, represents the union of intellect, speed, and simplicity, enabling enterprises to prosper in a world that is changing quickly. The road to digital greatness is easier to navigate as we keep learning about and using these tools. However, there are challenges along with benefits.

As technology develops, new avenues for human advancement and improvements in quality of life become possible. Techno-fusion will be the coming trend of merging exponential technologies into combined solutions. The neural interaction of AI and machine learning with quantum computing and super-computing power will enable unprecedented data mining, catalyze innovation, and provide the largest technological leap in human history.

Governments and businesses need to collaborate and build on those avenues to use technology for good. We may direct technologies to address global human difficulties, whether they are related to enhancing health care, optimizing our economic affairs, or managing pandemics, catastrophic fires, mudslides, or other existential concerns. The threats facing people are easy to identify and plan for, so we should prioritize contingencies. Technology has a plethora of applications that can benefit humanity. We must consider the significant roles that technologies—especially AI—play more expansively and cooperatively. In every emerging technology role, cybersecurity will continue to be a vital planning factor.

Notes

Chapter 1: An Overview of Our Merged Physical and Digital Worlds and Cybersecurity

1. Interaction Design Foundation. (n.d.). The Fourth Industrial Revolution. https://www.interaction-design.org/literature/topics/the-fourth-industrial-revolution
2. Cann, Oliver. (2016). $100 trillion by 2025: The digital dividend for society and business. https://www.weforum.org/press/2016/01/100-trillion-by-2025-the-digital-dividend-for-society-and-business/
3. Morgan, Steve. (2020). Cybercrime to cost the world $10.5 trillion by 2025. *Cybercrime Magazine*. https://cybersecurityventures.com/cybercrime-damages-6-trillion-by-2021/
4. Branka. (2024, February 17). Phishing statistics – 2024. https://truelist.co/blog/phishing-statistics/

Chapter 2: Cyber Threats, Targets, and Digital Convergence

1. Brenner, Joel. (2014). Nations everywhere are exploiting the lack of cybersecurity. Opinion. *Washington Post*. https://www.washingtonpost.com/opinions/joel-brenner-nations-everywhere-are-exploiting-the-lack-of-cybersecurity/2014/10/24/1e6e4b70-5b85-11e4-b812-38518ae74c67_story.html
2. Columbus, Louis. (2024). The five most alarming cyber threats from CrowdStrike's 2024 global threat report. VentureBeat. https://venturebeat.com/security/the-five-most-alarming-cyber-threats-from-crowdstrikes-2024-global-threat-report/
3. Statista. (n.d.). Annual number of data compromises and individuals impacted in the United States from 2005 to 2023. https://www.statista.com/statistics/273550/data-breaches-recorded-in-the-united-states-by-number-of-breaches-and-records-exposed/

4. YahooFinance. (2023). Cybersecurity burden falling "on consumers," not companies: CISA director. https://finance.yahoo.com/video/cybersecurity-burden-falling-consumers-not-220336148.html?guccounter=1

5. St. John, Mariah. (2024). Cybersecurity stats: Facts and figures you should know. *Forbes Advisor.* https://www.forbes.com/advisor/education/it-and-tech/cybersecurity-statistics/

Chapter 3: Common Cyber Threats and Defensive Tools

1. St. John, Mariah. (2024). Cybersecurity stats: Facts and figures you should know. *Forbes Advisor.* https://www.forbes.com/advisor/education/it-and-tech/cybersecurity-statistics/

2. Verizon. (2023). 2023 data breach investigations report. https://www.verizon.com/business/resources/reports/dbir/2023/master-guide/

3. Chainalysis. (2024). Ransomware payments exceed $1 billion in 2023, hitting record high after 2022 decline. https://www.chainalysis.com/blog/ransomware-2024/

4. Made in Britain. (n.d.). UK small businesses hit hardest by cyber-attacks. https://www.madeinbritain.org/news/uk-small-businesses-hit-hardest-by-cyber-attacks

5. Accenture. (2022, February 15). Cyber threat intelligence report. https://www.accenture.com/us-en/insights/security/cyber-threat-intelligence

6. Bitdefender. (2022, February 21). What are ransomware families? (And why knowing them can help your business avoid attack). https://www.bitdefender.com/blog/businessinsights/what-are-ransomware-families-and-why-knowing-them-can-help-your-business-avoid-attack/

7. National Cyber Security Centre (NCSC). (n.d.). Global ransomware threat expected to rise with AI, NCSC warns. https://www.ncsc.gov.uk/pdfs/news/global-ransomware-threat-expected-to-rise-with-ai.pdf

8. Cluley, Graham. (2024). NCSC warns that AI is already being used by ransomware gangs. Tripwire. https://www.tripwire.com/state-of-security/ncsc-warns-ai-already-being-used-ransomware-gangs?utm_source=The%20State%20of%20Security%20

Newsletter&utm_medium=email&utm_campaign=FO-01-29-2024&utm_content=httpswwwtripwirecomstateofsecurity ncscwarnsaialreadybeinginguseransomwaregangs&mkt_tok=MzE0LUlBSC03ODUAAAGQ-lceqZqnNH-Q1yscMlubuXqR3 pZ0RKfZCeJYtmTB5AsCWMUo47avBWg_Xf85Kb0BRUL fnRWDgVGoQbvYc5s51-3dxL0llBWa8pwaFy1OZR3d

9. Federal Bureau of Investigation. (n.d.). Ransomware. https://www.fbi.gov/how-we-can-help-you/scams-and-safety/common-scams-and-crimes/ransomware

10. NIST. (n.d.) Botnet. https://csrc.nist.gov/glossary/term/botnet

11. CSDE. (2019). International botnet and IOT security guide 2020. http://securingdigitaleconomy.org/wp-content/uploads/2019/11/CSDE_Botnet-Report_2020_FINAL.pdf

12. Woollacott, Emma. (2024). DDoS attacks are getting bigger and costlier—here's why. ITPro. https://www.itpro.com/security/ddos-attacks-are-getting-bigger-and-more-expensive-heres-why

Chapter 4: Cyber Threat Targets

1. Petrosyan, Ani. (2024, March 26). Annual number of supply chain cyber attacks in the United States from 2017 to 2023. https://www.statista.com/statistics/1367189/us-annual-number-of-supply-chain-attacks/

2. Boyens, Jon, Paulsen, Celia, Bartol, Nadya, Windler, Kris, & Gimbi, James. (2021). Key practices in cyber supply chain risk management: Observations from industry. https://nvlpubs.nist.gov/nistpubs/ir/2021/NIST.IR.8276.pdf

3. Information Security Forum. (n.d.). Managing the insider threat: Improving trustworthiness. https://www.securityforum.org/solutions-and-insights/managing-the-insider-threat-improving-trustworthiness/

4. Michalowski, Mariusz. (2024, March 27). 55 cloud computing statistics for 2024. https://spacelift.io/blog/cloud-computing-statistics

5. Duarte, Fabio. (2023). Amount of data created daily (2024). Exploding Topics. https://explodingtopics.com/blog/data-generated-per-day

6. Ikeda, Scott. (2021). DHS secretary: "Killware" malware designed to do real-world harm poised to be world's next breakout cybersecurity

threat. https://www.cpomagazine.com/cyber-security/dhs-secretary-killware-malware-designed-to-do-real-world-harm-poised-to-be-worlds-next-breakout-cybersecurity-threat/https://www.cpomagazine.com/cyber-security/dhs-secretary-killware-malware-designed-to-do-real-world-harm-poised-to-be-worlds-next-breakout-cybersecurity-threat/

7. World Economic Forum. (2024). Global risks report 2024. https://www.weforum.org/publications/global-risks-report-2024/

8. Easterly, Jen. (2024, May 29). A plan to protect critical infrastructure from 21st century threats. CISA. https://www.cisa.gov/news-events/news/plan-protect-critical-infrastructure-21st-century-threats

9. CISA. (n.d.). Critical infrastructure sections. https://www.cisa.gov/topics/critical-infrastructure-security-and-resilience/critical-infrastructure-sectors

10. Tal, Johnathan. (2018). America's critical infrastructure: Threats, vulnerabilities and solutions. https://www.securityinfowatch.com/access-identity/access-control/article/12427447/americas-critical-infrastructure-threats-vulnerabilities-and-solutions

Chapter 6: Artificial Intelligence

1. Gartner. (n.d.). What is artificial intelligence? https://www.gartner.com/en/topics/artificial-intelligence

2. MSPowerUser. (2016). Dave Coplin: AI is the most important technology that anybody on the planet is working on today. https://mspoweruser.com/dave-coplin-ai-important-technology-anybody-planet-working-today/

Chapter 9: Big Data and Data Analytics

1. Morgan, Steve. (2024). The world will store 200 zettabytes of data by 2025. https://cybersecurityventures.com/the-world-will-store-200-zettabytes-of-data-by-2025/

2. Eric Schmidt reports that "every two days we create as much information as we did up to 2003." (2010, August 4). Jeremy Norman's HistoryofInformation.com. https://www.historyofinformation.com/detail.php?entryid=3807

Chapter 10: Generative Artificial Intelligence

1. Panetta, Kassey. (2023). Set up now for AI to augment software development. Gartner. https://www.gartner.com/en/articles/set-up-now-for-ai-to-augment-software-development
2. Ibid.
3. Xu, Tammy. (2022, November 24). We could run out of data to train AI language programs. *MIT Technology Review*. https://www.technologyreview.com/2022/11/24/1063684/we-could-run-out-of-data-to-train-ai-language-programs/
4. Ibid.
5. The Atlas. (2024). The next wave. https://www.linkedin.com/pulse/next-wave-genai-works-km88f%3FtrackingId=44S4bTonv0u%252BORIEm2LRdg%253D%253D/?trackingId=44S4bTonv0u%2BORIEm2LRdg%3D%3D
6. Blackett, Phillip. (2024). AI revolutionizing supply chain management: Unlocking business scalability. LinkedIn. https://www.linkedin.com/pulse/ai-revolutionizing-supply-chain-management-unlocking-philip-blackett-khxqe/
7. Marr, Bernard. (2024). 10 mind-blowing generative AI stats everyone should know about. LinkedIn. https://www.linkedin.com/pulse/10-mind-blowing-generative-ai-stats-everyone-should-know-bernard-marr-kk48e/?midToken=AQHNhF6SaY2P2g&midSig=1VSd0aYGN2ib81&trk=eml-email_series_follow_newsletter_01-newsletter_content_preview-0-title_&trkEmail=eml-email_series_follow_newsletter_01-newsletter_content_preview-0-title_-null-2ws9f~lshp1jxd~9x-null-null&eid=2ws9f-lshp1jxd-9x&otpToken=MTYwZDE2ZTgxYTJiYzhjZWI1MjkwNWVkNDAxOGUwYjc4Y2M3ZDg0NDk5NDQ4ZTZlNzdjNzAyNmE0YzUwMzRmMGI1ZDBkN2JlNWFjYjc1YTEyMjAxNzI3YTQzNDUwMzAwYTTk1YWZlYzI5OGFmLDEsMQ%3D%3D

Chapter 11: The State of Artificial Intelligence and Smart Cybersecurity

1. CompTIA Community. (n.d.). IT industry outlook 2024. https://connect.comptia.org/content/research/it-industry-trends-analysis

2. Haan, Katherine, & Watts, Rob. (2023). How businesses are using artificial intelligence in 2024. *Forbes.* https://www.forbes.com/ advisor/business/software/ai-in-business/

3. Campbell, Scott. (2023). How to use machine learning and AI in your business. CompTIA. https://www.comptia.org/blog/how-to-use-machine-learning-and-ai-in-your-business

4. Thomas, Mike, updated by Whitfield, Brennan. (2024). 12 risks and dangers of artificial intelligence (AI). Built In. https://builtin .com/artificial-intelligence/risks-of-artificial-intelligence

5. Maheshwari, Rashi. (2024). Top AI statistics and trends. *Forbes.* https://www.forbes.com/advisor/in/business/ai-statistics/

6. Duarte, Fabio. (2024). AI market size statistics (2024). Exploding Topics. https://explodingtopics.com/blog/ai-market-size-stats

7. Markets and Markets. (2023). Artificial intelligence market worth $407.0 billion by 2027, growing at a CAGR of 36.2%. Global News Wire. https://www.globenewswire.com/en/news-release/2023/05/ 17/2671170/0/en/Artificial-Intelligence-Market-Worth-407-0-Billion-By-2027-Growing-At-A-CAGR-Of-36-2-Report-By-MarketsandMarkets.html#:~:text=Chicago%2C%20May%20 17%2C%202023%20(,new%20report%20by%20Marketsand Markets%E2%84%A2

8. Precedence Research. (n.d.). Artificial intelligence market. https:// www.precedenceresearch.com/artificial-intelligence-market

9. CompTIA Community. (n.d.). Artificial intelligence in business: Top considerations before implementing AI. https://connect .comptia.org/content/guides/business-considerations-before-implementing-ai/

10. IBM Newsroom. (2022). Global data from IBM shows steady AI adoption as organizations look to address skills shortages, automate processes and encourage sustainable operations. https:// newsroom.ibm.com/2022-05-19-Global-Data-from-IBM-Shows-Steady-AI-Adoption-as-Organizations-Look-to-Address-Skills-Short ages,-Automate-Processes-and-Encourage-Sustainable-Operations

11. Capgemini Research Institute. (n.d.). Generative AI in organiza-tions. https://www.capgemini.com/insights/research-library/gene rative-ai-in-organizations/

12. Simon, Charles. (2022). As AI advances, will human workers disappear? *Forbes.* https://www.forbes.com/sites/forbestechcouncil/2022/06/28/as-ai-advances-will-human-workers-disappear/?sh=3c7b01b15e68

13. Glasner, Joanna. (2023). AI's share of US startup funding doubled in 2023. *Crunchbase News.*

14. IBM Newsroom. (2022).

15. Wardini, Josh. (2024). 101 Artificial intelligence statistics. Tech Jury. https://techjury.net/blog/ai-statistics/

16. Omale, Gloria. (2019). Gartner predicts 25 percent of digital workers will use virtual employee assistants daily by 2021. Gartner. https://www.gartner.com/en/newsroom/press-releases/2019-01-09-gartner-predicts-25-percent-of-digital-workers-will-u

17. GO-Globe. (2018). The rise of virtual digital assistants usage—Statistics and trends. https://www.go-globe.com/the-rise-of-virtual-digital-assistants-usage-statistics-and-trends/

18. Bleu, Nicola. (2024). 29 top chatbot statistics for 2024: Usage, demographics, trends. Blogging Wizard. https://bloggingwizard.com/chatbot-statistics/

19. Jones, Padrig. (2024). 78 artificial intelligence statistics and trends for 2024. Semrush Blog. https://www.semrush.com/blog/artificial-intelligence-stats/

20. Matzelle, Emily. (2024). Top artificial intelligence statistics and facts for 2024. CompTIA Community. https://connect.comptia.org/blog/artificial-intelligence-statistics-facts

Chapter 12: How Artificial Intelligence Can Help Cybersecurity

1. Conner-Simmons, Adam. (2016). Could artificial intelligence help us predict cyber attacks more accurately? World Economic Forum. https://www.weforum.org/agenda/2016/04/could-artificial-intelligence-help-us-predict-cyber-attacks-more-accurately/

2. Dignan, Larry. (2016, September 27). Automation, AI among key takeaways for security execs, ecosystem. ZDNET. https://www.zdnet.com/article/automation-ai-among-key-takeaways-for-security-execs-ecosystem/

3. Korolov, Maria. (2024). How gen AI helps entry-level SOC analysts improve their skills. CSO. https://www.csoonline.com/article/1310938/how-genai-helps-entry-level-soc-analysts-improve-their-skills.html?utm_date=20240318170040&utm_campaign=CSO%20US%20First%20Look&utm_content=Slot%20One%20Read%20More%3A%20By%20automating%20repetitive%20triage%20and%20documentation%20tasks%2C%20generative%20AI%20systems%20allow%20entry-level%20security%20analysts%20to%20spend%20more%20time%20on%20investigations%2C%20response%2C%20and%20developing%20core%20skills.&utm_term=CSO%20US%20Editorial%20Newsletters&utm_medium=email&utm_source=Adestra&huid=040100f5-bc13-4688-af2b-08a56480a80e
4. Columbus, Louis. (2024). Eight emerging areas of opportunity for AI in security. Venture Beat. https://venturebeat.com/security/eight-emerging-areas-of-opportunity-for-ai-in-security/
5. Reisinger, Don. (2024). Google survey: 63% of IT and security pros believe AI will improve corporate cybersecurity. ZDNet. https://www.zdnet.com/article/ai-should-improve-corporate-cybersecurity-google-and-csa-survey-finds/
6. Ennis, Gail S. (2023). Letter to Senator Bob Casey. https://oig.ssa.gov/assets/uploads/2023-11-16_modern-scams-how-scammers-are-using-artificial-intelligence-and-how-we-can-fight-back_gail-s-ennis.pdf
7. Microsoft. (2024). Navigating cyberthreats and strengthening defenses in the era of AI. Cyber Signals. https://www.microsoft.com/en-us/security/business/security-insider/wp-content/uploads/2024/02/cyber-signals-issue-6.pdf

Chapter 13: The Other Side of the Artificial Intelligence Cyber Coin

1. Microsoft Threat Intelligence. (2024). Staying ahead of threat actors in the age of AI. https://www.microsoft.com/en-us/security/blog/2024/02/14/staying-ahead-of-threat-actors-in-the-age-of-ai/?ranMID=24542&ranEAID=nOD/rLJHOac&ranSiteID=nOD_rLJHOac-3SJ6xQeat7sAXW6FAsLpKQ&epi=nOD_rLJHOac-3SJ6xQeat7sAXW6FAsLpKQ&irgwc=1&OCID=AIDcmm549zy

227_aff_7593_1243925&tduid=%28ir__i2ohkh1nogkfdgz0zoybu2s
yk32x9tv6ml3hilof00%29%287593%29%281243925%29%28nOD_
rLJHOac-3SJ6xQeat7sAXW6FAsLpKQ%29%28%29&irclickid=_
i2ohkh1nogkfdgz0zoybu2syk32x9tv6ml3hilof00; French, Laura.
(2024). Microsoft, OpenAI reveal ChatGPT use by state-sponsored
hackers.   https://www.scmagazine.com/news/microsoft-openai-
reveal-chatgpt-use-by-state-sponsored-hackers?nbd=q-ziIno
B12oGuDO_0zmn&nbd_source=mrkto&mkt_tok=MTg4LVVOWi
02NjAAAAGRSH-yCuktdOtompy-bOhKBr_g-EzfxJqwZcg5JbFEBeL
ErmgMRQEMV0nSUyss-VtEK5Q_7k5IeH_dpzDaBLKEUBBXwR
dunD34B8KD9VBxGw

2. Nguyen, Britney. (2024). Cyber attackers are using AI to get better, Microsoft executive says. Quartz. https://qz.com/business-cyberattacks-ai-threat-microsoft-1851329563

3. Paganini, Pierluigi. (2023). FraudGPT, a new malicious generative AI tool appears in the threat landscape. https://securityaffairs.com/148829/cyber-crime/fraudgpt-cybercrime-generative-ai.html

4. Acronis. (2023). Acronis cyberthreats report, H2 2023: Alarming rise in cyberattacks, SMBs and MSPs in the crosshairs. https://www.acronis.com/en-us/resource-center/resource/acronis-cyberthreats-report-h2-2023/

5. GlobalNewswire. (2024). Acronis announced findings of cyberthreats report of second half of 2023. https://ai-techpark.com/acronis-announced-findings-of-cyberthreats-report-for-second-half-2023/

6. Columbus, Louis. (2023). Experts predict how AI will energize cybersecurity in 2023 and beyond. https://venturebeat.com/security/experts-predict-how-ai-will-energize-cybersecurity-in-2023-and-beyond/

7. Ibid.

8. Rathnayake, Dilki. (2024). Cybersecurity in the age of AI: Exploring AI-generated cyber attacks. Fortra. https://www.tripwire.com/state-of-security/cybersecurity-age-ai-exploring-ai-generated-cyber-attacks

9. Security Staff. (2024). 55% of generative AI inputs comprised personally identifiable data. *Security*. https://www.securitymagazine.com/articles/100400-55-of-generative-ai-inputs-comprised-personally-identifiable-data

10. Help Net Security. (2024). 22% of employees admit to breaching company rules with GenAI. https://www.helpnetsecurity.com/ 2024/04/05/employee-security-productivity-balance/

11. Johnson, Dave, & Johnson, Alexander. (2023). What are deep-fakes? How fake AI-powered audio and video warps our perception of reality. Business Insider. https://www.businessinsider.com/ guides/tech/what-is-deepfake

12. French, Laura. (2024). Deepfake face swap attacks on ID verification systems up 704% in 2023. https://www.scmagazine.com/ news/deepfake-face-swap-attacks-on-id-verification-systems-up-704-in-2023?nbd=q-ziInoB12oGuDO_0zmn&nbd_source=mrkto&mkt_tok=MTg4LVVOWi02NjAAAAGRQU_DTT1Y 9PqPqSvsSUNcc32qCgf3Qv2JXDN3QUwDL2F3oePyLIKYpzyg XAu-uKzsoZSTq3wURzcfAHm8pFnZIk-zMb4b3uM0LDyhIBkBCA

13. RTHK. (2024). Deepfake colleagues trick HK clerk into paying HK$200m. https://news.rthk.hk/rthk/en/component/k2/1739119-20240204.htm

14. Versprille, Allyson. (2024). AI is making financial fraud easier and more sophisticated, US Treasury warns. *Moody's*. https://www .bloomberg.com/news/articles/2024-03-27/impersonation-phishing-getting-trickier-with-ai-treasury-warns?leadSource= uverify%20wall

15. Edwards, Benj. (2024). OpenAI holds back wide release of voice-cloning tech due to misuse concerns. Ars Technica. https:// arstechnica.com/information-technology/2024/03/openai-holds-back-wide-release-of-voice-cloning-tech-due-to-misuse-concerns/

16. Villasenor, John. (2019). Artificial intelligence, deepfakes, and the uncertain future of truth. Brookings. https://www.brookings.edu/ articles/artificial-intelligence-deepfakes-and-the-uncertain-future-of-truth/

17. National Cyber Security Centre. (2024). The near-term impact of AI on the cyber threat. https://www.ncsc.gov.uk/report/impact-of-ai-on-cyber-threat

18. Riskonnect (n.d.). The new generation of risk: Are you ahead of the curve or behind the pack? https://riskonnect.com/reports/ new-generation-of-risk-ahead-of-the-curve-or-behind-the-pack/

Chapter 14: Responding to Artificial Intelligence Cyber Threats

1. Stanham, Lucia. (2023). Machine learning (ML) in cybersecurity: Use cases. CrowdStrike. https://www.crowdstrike.com/cyberse curity-101/machine-learning-cybersecurity/
2. Google. (2024). Secure, empower, advance: How AI can reverse the defender's dilemma. https://services.google.com/fh/files/ misc/how-ai-can-reverse-defenders-dilemma.pdf
3. Kramer, Shelly. (2024). Four generative AI cyber risks that keep CISOs up at night—and how to combat them. SiliconANGLE. https://siliconangle.com/2024/03/24/four-generative-ai-cyber-risks-keep-cisos-night-combat/
4. Harper, Jon. (2024). DARPA transitions new technology to shield military AI systems from trickery. DefenseScoop. https://defenses coop.com/2024/03/27/darpa-transitions-tech-gard-program-cdao/
5. Gottsegen, Gordon. (2023). How machine learning in cybersecurity works. BuiltIn. https://builtin.com/artificial-intelligence/ machine-learning-cybersecurity
6. Binns, Rob. (2024, March 29). AI names 2024's biggest cybersecurity threats – and AI is one of them. https://www.techopedia .com/ai-names-biggest-cybersecurity-threats

Chapter 15: Artificial Intelligence and Privacy

1. Kennedy, John. (2013, November 21). Father of the internet Vint Cerf: "Privacy may be an anomaly." Siliconrepublic. https://www .siliconrepublic.com/comms/father-of-the-internet-vint-cerf-privacy-may-be-an-anomaly
2. Solove, Daniel J. (2024). Artificial intelligence and privacy. *Florida Law Review* (forthcoming 2025). https://papers.ssrn.com/ sol3/papers.cfm?abstract_id=4713111
3. Southwick, Ron. (2023), Healthcare cyberattacks have affected more than 100 million people in 2023. Chief Healthcare Executive. https://www.chiefhealthcareexecutive.com/view/health-data-cyberattacks-have-affected-more-than-100-million-people-in-2023
4. Sullivan, Morgan. (2024). AI and your privacy: Understanding the concerns. Transcend. https://transcend.io/blog/ai-privacy-issues

Chapter 16: Artificial Intelligence and Ethics

1. Ajao, Ester. (2023) A look at writers' battle to get AI vendors to pay them. TechTarget. https://www.techtarget.com/searchenterpriseai/news/366544611/A-look-at-writers-battle-to-get-AI-vendors-to-pay-them

2. Connor, James. (2024). The intersection of AI capabilities and ethics: Computer vision and cognitive warfare. LinkedIn. https://www.linkedin.com/pulse/intersection-ai-capabilities-ethics-computer-vision-cognitive-connor-wsbhc/

3. UN News. (2024). General Assembly adopts landmark resolution on artificial intelligence. https://news.un.org/en/story/2024/03/1147831

4. Thomas, Mike. (2024). The future of AI: How AI is changing the world. Built In. https://builtin.com/artificial-intelligence/artificial-intelligence-future

5. European Commission. (2021). Proposal for a regulation of the European Parliament and of the Council Laying Down Harmonised Rules on Artificial Intelligence (Artificial Intelligence Act) and amending certain union legislative acts. EUR-Lex. https://eur-lex.europa.eu/legal-content/EN/TXT/?uri=CELEX:52021PC0206

6. The White House. (2023). Fact sheet: President Biden issues executive order on safe, secure, and trustworthy artificial intelligence. https://www.whitehouse.gov/briefing-room/statements-releases/2023/10/30/fact-sheet-president-biden-issues-executive-order-on-safe-secure-and-trustworthy-artificial-intelligence/

7. Department of Homeland Security. (2024). Artificial intelligence roadmap 2024. https://www.dhs.gov/sites/default/files/2024-03/24_0315_ocio_roadmap_artificialintelligence-ciov3-signed-508.pdf

8. Cantwell, Helen V., et. al. (2024). DOJ announces initiative to combat AI-assisted crimes. Debevoise & Plimpton Data Blog. https://www.debevoisedatablog.com/2024/02/16/doj-announces-initiative-to-combat-ai-assisted-crime/

9. US Department of Justice. (2024, February 16). FACT SHEET: Disruptive technology strike force efforts in first year to prevent sensitive technology from being acquired by authoritarian regimes and hostile nation-states. Press release. https://www.justice.gov/opa/pr/fact-sheet-disruptive-technology-strike-force-efforts-first-year-prevent-sensitive

10. The White House. (2023). FACT SHEET: Biden-Harris Administration secures voluntary commitments from leading artificial voluntary commitments—underscoring safety, security, and trust—mark a critical step toward developing responsible AI. https://www.whitehouse.gov/briefing-room/statements-releases/2023/07/21/fact-sheet-biden-harris-administration-secures-voluntary-commitments-from-leading-artificial-intelligence-companies-to-manage-the-risks-posed-by-ai/

11. Tucci, Linda, & Karjian, Ron. (n.d.). Chief digital officer. TechTarget. https://www.techtarget.com/searchcio/definition/Chief-Digital-Officer-CDO

12. Rose, Scott W, Borchert, Oliver, Mitchell, Stuart, & Connelly, Sean. (2010, August 10). *Zero trust architecture*. NIST. https://www.nist.gov/publications/zero-trust-architecture

13. Chief Digital and Artificial Intelligence Office (CDAO). https://www.ai.mil/

14. Fabbro, Rocio. (2024). Jamie Dimon says interest rates could hit 8% "or even more" and other highlights from his annual letter. Quartz. https://qz.com/jamie-dimon-jpmorgan-chase-ai-interest-rates-economy-1851394989

15. https://mkaku.org/home/publications/about-the-future-of-the-mind/

16. McKinsey Digital. (2020, August 12). *How six companies are using technology and data to transform themselves*. https://www.mckinsey.com/capabilities/mckinsey-digital/our-insights/how-six-companies-are-using-technology-and-data-to-transform-themselves

17. Ibid.

18. Intelligent Computing. (2024). Affective computing: Scientists connect human emotions with AI. https://scitechdaily.com/affective-computing-scientists-connect-human-emotions-with-ai/

19. Tangermann, Victor. (2023). Scientists preparing to turn on computer intended to simulate entire human brain. https://futurism.com/the-byte/scientists-computer-neural-human-brain

20. Afifi-Sabet, Keumars. (2024, March 6). AI singularity may come in 2027 with artificial "super intelligence" sooner than we thing, says top scientist. LiveScience. https://www.livescience.com/technology/artificial-intelligence/ai-agi-singularity-in-2027-artificial-super-intelligence-sooner-than-we-think-ben-goertzel

21. Kurzwel, Ray. (2005). *The singularity is near: When humans transcend biology* (Viking Press).

22. Phelan, Matthew. (2024). Top scientist warns AI could surpass human intelligence by 2027—decades earlier than previously predicted. *Daily Mail*. https://www.dailymail.co.uk/sciencetech/article-13165581/top-scientist-ai-surpass-human-intelligence-2027.html

23. Deloitte. (2019). Artificial intelligence: The next frontier for investment management firms. fsi-artificial-intelligence-investment-mgmt

24. Goldman Sachs. (2023). AI investment forecast to approach $200 billion globally by 2025. https://www.goldmansachs.com/intelligence/pages/ai-investment-forecast-to-approach-200-billion-globally-by-2025.html

25. Reuters. (2024). Microsoft, OpenAI plan $100 billion data-center project, media report says. https://www.reuters.com/technology/microsoft-openai-planning-100-billion-data-center-project-information-reports-2024-03-29/

26. Farrell, Maureen, & Copeland, Rob. (2024). Saudi Arabia plans $40 billion push into artificial intelligence. *New York Times*. https://www.nytimes.com/2024/03/19/business/saudi-arabia-investment-artificial-intelligence.html

27. Lindrea, Brayden. (2024). Trudeau announces $1.8B package to boost Canada's AI sector. Cointelegraph. https://cointelegraph.com/news/canada-justin-trudeau-federal-package-budget-boost-ai-sector

28. Gulen, Kerem. (2022). Artificial intelligence as the cornerstone of emerging technologies. Dataconomy. https://dataconomy.com/2022/09/06/emerging-technologies-artificial-intelligence/

29. Nichols, Greg. (2021). 2022: A major revolution in robotics. ZDNet. https://www.zdnet.com/article/2022-prediction-a-major-revolution-in-robotics/

30. Chadwick, Jonathan. (2022). Terminator-style robot can survive being STABBED. *Daily Mail*. https://www.dailymail.co.uk/sciencetech/article-11520519/Terminator-style-robot-survive-STABBED.html

31. Ghose, Tia. (2013). Intelligent robots will overtake humans by 2100, experts say. Live Science. https://www.livescience.com/29379-intelligent-robots-will-overtake-humans.html

Chapter 17: The Interface Between Humans and Computers

1. Best, Jo. (2020). What is neuromorphic computing? Everything you need to know about how it is changing the future of computing. ZDNet.https://www.zdnet.com/article/what-is-neuromorphic-computing-everything-you-need-to-know-about-how-it-will-change-the-future-of-computing/

2. Broback, Steve. (n.d.). Can computers make humans "super"? Innovation & Tech Today. https://innotechtoday.com/can-technology-make-humans-super/

3. Transformational science for healthy lives on a healthy planet. (n.d.). *Frontiers in Science.* https://www.frontiersin.org/journals/science

4. Martins, Nuno R. B., et al. (2019). Human brain/cloud interface. *Frontiers in Neuroscience* 13. https://doi.org/10.3389/fnins.2019.00112

5. Hern, Alex. (2024, January 30). Elon Musk says Neuralink has implanted its first brain chip in human. *The Guardian.* https://www.theguardian.com/technology/2024/jan/29/elon-musk-neuralink-first-human-brain-chip-implant

6. Grimes, Brittney. (2022). Artificial neural network: Here's everything you need to know about black box of AI. *Interesting Engineering.* https://interestingengineering.com/innovation/artificial-neural-network-black-box-ai

7. Yang, Y., Yuan, Y., Zhang, G., et al. (2022). Artificial intelligence-enabled detection and assessment of Parkinson's disease using nocturnal breathing signals. *Nature Medicine, 28*, 2207–2215. https://doi.org/10.1038/s41591-022-01932-x

8. Greenmeier, Larry. (2014). Brain-inspired computing reaches a new milestone. *Scientific American.* https://www.scientificamerican.com/blog/observations/brain-inspired-computing-reaches-a-new-milestone/

9. Caughill, Patrick. (2017). Ray Kurzweil's most exciting predictions about the future of humanity. Futurism. https://futurism.com/ray-kurzweils-most-exciting-predictions-about-the-future-of-humanity

10. Grozinger, L., Amos, M., Gorochowski, T. E., et al. (2019). Pathways to cellular supremacy in biocomputing. *Nature Communications, 10*, 5250. https://doi.org/10.1038/s41467-019-13232-z
11. Brooks, Chuck. (2019). The new techno-fusion: The merging of technologies impacting our future. *Forbes*. https://www.forbes.com/sites/cognitiveworld/2019/02/26/the-new-techno-fusion-the-merging-of-technologies-impacting-our-future/?sh=3b504fc91f3e

Chapter 18: Artificial Intelligence and Health Care

1. Davis, Steve, et. al. (2024). Public health's inflection point with generative AI. McKinsey. https://www.mckinsey.com/industries/social-sector/our-insights/public-healths-inflection-point-with-generative-ai

Chapter 19: The Internet of Things

1. Adshead, Antony. (2017). Analytics, internet of things to drive data volumes to 163ZB by 2025. *Computer Weekly*. https://www.computerweekly.com/news/450416206/Analytics-internet-of-things-to-drive-data-volumes-to-163ZB-by-2025
2. eeNewsEurope. (2013). Janusz Bryzek: The trillion-sensor man: Part 1. https://www.eenewseurope.com/en/janusz-bryzek-the-trillion-sensor-man-part-1/
3. Ghosh, Iman. (2020). AIoT: When artificial intelligence meets the Internet of Things. Visual Capitalist. https://www.visualcapitalist.com/aiot-when-ai-meets-iot-technology/
4. Husar, Alex. (2022). IoT security: 5 cyber-attacks caused by IoT security vulnerabilities. Cyber Management. https://www.cm-alliance.com/cybersecurity-blog/iot-security-5-cyber-attacks-caused-by-iot-security-vulnerabilities
5. United States Government Accountability Office. (2020). Internet of Things: Information on use by federal agencies. https://www.gao.gov/assets/gao-20-577.pdf
6. The World Bank. (2023). Urban development overview. https://www.worldbank.org/en/topic/urbandevelopment/overview

Chapter 20: 5G

1. *VA News*. (2020). VA Palo Alto first 5G hospital. https://news.va
.gov/72556/va-palo-alto-first-5g-hospital/

Chapter 21: Quantum Computing

1. Panetta, Kasey. (2019). The CIO's guide to quantum computing.
Gartner. https://www.gartner.com/smarterwithgartner/the-cios-
guide-to-quantum-computing
2. Gil, Dario. (2020). Quantum computing may be closer than you
think. *Scientific American*. https://www.scientificamerican.com/
article/quantum-computing-may-be-closer-than-you-think/
3. Dungey, Trinity, et al. (2022). Quantum computing: Current
progress and future directions. *Educause Review*. https://
er.educause.edu/articles/2022/7/quantum-computing-current-
progress-and-future-directions
4. Diamandis, Peter H. (2018, August 22). Ray Kurzweil's mind-
boggling predictions for the next 25 years. Medium. https://
medium.com/@singularity_41680/ray-kurzweils-mind-boggling-
predictions-for-the-next-25-years-ce3c9163588b
5. Swayne, Matt. (2022). Photonic link could spark an all-silicon
quantum internet, scalable quantum devices. The Quantum Insider.
https://thequantuminsider.com/2022/07/18/photonic-link-could-
spark-an-all-silicon-quantum-internet-scalable-quantum-devices/
6. Suleyman, Mustafa. (2023). How the AI revolution will reshape
the world. *Time*. https://time.com/6310115/ai-revolution-reshape-
the-world/

Chapter 22: Quantum Technologies and Cybersecurity

1. Booz Allen Hamilton. (n.d.). Chinese threats in the quantum era.
https://www.boozallen.com/expertise/analytics/quantum-
computing/chinese-cyber-threats-in-the-quantum-era.html
2. *Financial Times*. (n.d.). Chinese researchers claim to find way to
break encryption using quantum computers. https://www.ft.com/
content/b15680c0-cf31-448d-9eb6-b30426c29b8b

3. Waugh, Rob. (2023). The quantum apocalypse—when encryption banking stops working and the world's savings could evaporate—is "just YEARS away." *Daily Mail*. https://www.dailymail.co.uk/sciencetech/article-11628963/The-Quantum-Apocalypse-just-YEARS-away-experts-say.html

4. Kery, Tim. (2023). IBM: Quantum computing poses an "existential threat" to data encryption. VentureBeat. https://venturebeat.com/security/ibm-quantum-computing/

5. Brooks, Chuck. (2022). The quantum era is arriving and it will be transformational! *Forbes*. https://www.forbes.com/sites/chuckbrooks/2022/07/20/the-quantum-era-is-arriving-and-it-will-be-transformational-/?sh=3089b82f4e7a

6. Brooks, Chuck. (2023). Artificial intelligence, quantum computing, and space are 3 tech areas to watch in 2024. *Forbes*. https://www.forbes.com/sites/chuckbrooks/2023/12/12/artificial-intelligence-quantum-computing-and-space-are-3-tech-areas-to-watch-in-2024/?sh=690beb8b6796

7. Mitobe, Mutsumi. (2023). First quantum computer made in Japan by Riken put online. The Asahi Shimbun. https://www.asahi.com/ajw/articles/14871014

8. *Japan Times*. (2022). Tokyo proposes first domestic quantum computer use by March 2023. https://www.japantimes.co.jp/news/2022/04/07/business/tech/domestic-quantum-computer-plan/

Chapter 23: Quantum Internet of Things

1. Dolan, Shelagh. (2019). How the Internet of Things will transform consumerism, enterprises, and governments over the next five years. Business Insider India. https://www.businessinsider.in/tech/news/how-the-internet-of-things-will-transform-consumerism-enterprises-and-governments-over-the-next-five-years/articleshow/72240440.cms

2. 4.0 Research. (2024). Quantum computing market & technologies 2018–2024. industry40marketresearch.com

3. Mastery, Torry. (n.d.). Quantum computing: Top ten things you need to know. *DotCom Magazine*. https://dotcommagazine.com/2024/03/quantum-computing-top-ten-things-you-need-to-know-2/

4. McKinsey & Company. (2024, April 24). Steady progress in approaching the quantum advantage. https://www.mckinsey.com/capabilities/mckinsey-digital/our-insights/steady-progress-in-approaching-the-quantum-advantage

Chapter 24: The Holy Digital Grail

1. Capers, Zach. (2024). 2024 tech trends: How fast-growing businesses will buy more software (and regret it later). Gartner Digital Markets. https://www.gartner.com/en/digital-markets/insights/2024-tech-trends-fast-growing-businesses

Chapter 25: The Urgency of Having a Cyber Risk Management Plan

1. US Securities and Exchange Commission. (2023). SEC adopts rules on cybersecurity risk management, strategy, governance, and incident disclosure by public companies. https://www.sec.gov/news/press-release/2023-139
2. Cybersecurity & Infrastructure Security Agency. (2023). Secure-by-design. https://www.cisa.gov/resources-tools/resources/secure-by-design?utm_source=Blog&utm_medium=CISA.gov&utm_campaign=Secure%20by%20Design%20and%20Default%20Update
3. Mell, Peter M., Shook, James, & Harang, Richard. (2017). Measuring and improving the effectiveness of defense-in-depth postures. NIST. https://www.nist.gov/publications/measuring-and-improving-effectiveness-defense-depth-postures
4. Cybersecurity & Infrastructure Security Agency. (n.d.). Joint cyber defense collaborative. https://www.cisa.gov/topics/partnerships-and-collaboration/joint-cyber-defense-collaborative

Acknowledgments

Special thanks to the great team of editors at Wiley Publishing, who really know the craft of literary creation and guided me throughout.

A special nod to Dr. Frederic Lemieux of Georgetown University, who encouraged me to create and teach a course on disruptive technologies in the graduate cybersecurity risk management program. From teaching and learning I have continually expanded my knowledge of the digital era.

And to my many colleagues who I had the pleasure of working with in both government and industry over the years, including Dr. Thomas Cellucci, Chris Skroupa, Admiral Jay Cohen, Pam Turner, Chuck McQueary, Hon. Curt Weldon, John Gallagher, Karen Firkser, Scott Arthur, Dennis Pollutro, Yoon Ji, Bob Liscouski, Mitchell Scherr, George Platsis, Monte Brown, Luke Bencie, Rob Wynne, Adam Emanuel, Paul Goldenberg, Ira Hoffman, Marc Burchman, Martin Tang, Tyler Cohen Wood, Scott Schober, Ludmila Morozova-Buss, Jo Peterson, Dr. Rebecca Wynn, and the late Marvin Josephson, late Yoram Hessel, late Steve Trevino, and late Paul Michael Wihbey.

And to all the great cybersecurity leaders out there working tirelessly to help secure our networks and devices.

About the Author

Chuck Brooks serves as president of Brooks Consulting International. He also serves as an adjunct professor at Georgetown University, teaching graduate courses on risk management, emerging technologies, and cybersecurity.

Chuck was named "Top 5 Tech Person to Follow" by LinkedIn, where he has 117,000 followers on his profile. As a thought leader, blogger, and event speaker, he has briefed the G20 on energy cybersecurity and the US Embassy to the Holy See and Vatican on global cybersecurity cooperation. He has served on two National Academy of Science Advisory groups, including one on digitalizing the USAF and another on securing biotech. He has also addressed USTRANSCOM on cybersecurity and serves on an industry/government working group for CISA focused on security space systems.

Chuck is also a contributor to *Forbes*, the *Washington Post*, Dark Reading, *Homeland Security Today*, Security Information, Skytop Media, GovCon, *Barrons*, *The Hill*, and *Federal Times* on cybersecurity and emerging technology topics.

Chuck has received presidential appointments for executive service by two US presidents, including appointments to the Department of Homeland Security and Voice of America and served in executive leadership roles at public companies General Dynamics, Xerox, and Rapiscan.

He has an MA from the University of Chicago, a BA from DePauw University, and a certificate in international law from The Hague Academy of International Law.

Index